DOLLY PARTON
Biography

The Story of Dreams and Determination

Christopher Andrew Telencio

Copyright © 2023
All rights reserved.

The content of this book may not be reproduced, duplicated, or transmitted without the author's or publisher's express written permission. Under no circumstances will the publisher or author be held liable or legally responsible for any damages, reparation, or monetary loss caused by the information contained in this book, whether directly or indirectly.

Legal Notice:

This publication is copyrighted. It is strictly for personal use only. You may not change, distribute, sell, use, quote, or paraphrase any part of this book without the author's or publisher's permission.

Disclaimer Notice:

Please keep in mind that the information in this document is only for educational and entertainment purposes. Every effort has been made to present accurate, up-to-date, reliable, and comprehensive information. There are no express or implied warranties. Readers understand that the author is not providing legal, financial, medical, or professional advice. This book's content was compiled from a variety of sources. Please seek the advice of a licensed professional before attempting any of the techniques described in this book. By reading this document, the reader agrees that the author is not liable for any direct or indirect losses incurred as a result of using the information contained within this document, including, but not limited to, errors, omissions, or inaccuracies.

TABLE OF CONTENTS

Introduction

Chapter 1: Embodies The Working Woman's Fight
Outta That Holler
Talking Through Songs
The Last Laugh

Chapter 2: Masters The Art Of Leaving
Leaving Home
Having Enough
Escape Artists
An Open Door
Punching Out

Chapter 3: Becomes The Boss
Feminist Sweet Spot
Body Politics
The Freedom To Work

Chapter 4: Cements Her Icon Status
Giving Back
Big Business
Hits And Misses

Nip It, Tuck It, Suck It

So Much Substance

God's Little Dolly Parton

Don't Need No Company

INTRODUCTION

If you have any doubts about how far women have come in the century since they were granted the right to vote in 1920, just think of Dolly Parton, a modern-day phenomenon.

Instead of using the word "feminist" to declare her authority, she dresses up female torsos like T-shirts and declares her dominance with a massive head of hair. She is shown with a halo and burns on desks as a profane prayer candle (over a huge mound of hair). She routinely speaks on talk shows and award-show platforms, where older women have traditionally been underrepresented, even though she is well into her seventies.

People can't get enough of Dolly, who is now a widely adored figure acknowledged as a creative genius with a goddess-sized heart, as attested by hagiographic magazine pieces, feverish tweets, and diverse, roaring audiences.

She used to be mostly recognized by many people as the punchline of a joke.

So why the sudden change in attitude?

Women's suffrage had been secured by a US constitutional amendment just twenty-six years earlier, when Parton was born into rural poverty in 1946. A system in which the female body had few protections from assault, unplanned pregnancy, or discounted work resulted in widespread maltreatment of women notwithstanding the recent economic advancements they had made in the midst of a wartime economy. Women in poverty and women of color fared the worst because of societal institutions that privilege wealth and whiteness, coming out on the losing end. Their efforts to advance gender equality, however, were unappreciated, unrecorded, and misunderstood.

Young Parton fled her Appalachian holler in the 1960s with independent goals that bucked gender stereotypes despite her lack of formal education. She accomplished her goals, freeing herself from the constraints of men's decisions, men's money, and men's everything, like so many other women of her day. Like so many others, she was also gravely misjudged and devalued along the road.

Parton was a great force—not just in songwriting and singing but in gender presentation and business—even though she was pitched as a smiling "girl singer" at the start of her career and referenced primarily by her physical characteristics for decades to come. Many of her fans in the twenty-first century are thus "discovering" what was there all along, hidden but for the patriarchal blinders: Parton's artistry, intellectual depth, and self-made paradoxes that subtly critique our nation's long-denied caste system (looking "cheap," for example, while by all accounts acting with pure class).

Parton does not identify as a "feminist," and, like me, she comes from a background where "theory" is really an educated guess as to how the coyotes manage to break into the chicken coop time and time again. I'm convinced that her long-standing propensity to perform when dressed entirely in white is not a tribute to suffragists. Her work, however, is a nod to the women who are working with their bodies while others are tweeting with their fingers—those who cannot afford to fly to the march.

The issues of gender and economic status are still relevant today, with another election year and a volatile political environment. But there is much more to this story than that. The story revolves about leaving yet never truly leaving home. It's about a quality that is unfashionable in our irate society—grace—and how it may motivate people to be their best selves. As she plays the fiddle, a hot young cowboy is instructed to dance in place by a 70-year-old woman.

Then, the racial controversy in Parton's close vicinity was her decades-old Dixie Stampede dinner theater tourist attraction, which portrayed the Civil War as foolish, whitewashed entertainment; in response to criticism, the Parton-owned company withdrew the "Dixie" from its name in 2018. Currently, the pervasive Black Lives Matter movement is forcing a national reckoning in public policy and beyond after video of George Floyd's murder at the hands of law enforcement in May 2020 sparked worldwide protests against police brutality and systemic racism. This is forcing celebrities to make decisions about how to use their cultural influence.

Many country music celebrities have shown their support. As demonstrators around the nation toppled monuments honoring slave owners, Faith Hill, for example, demanded that the Confederate "stars and bars" be removed from the state flag of Mississippi, the state of her birth. The multi-platinum-selling trio the Dixie Chicks, who went by "The Chicks" and released a daring protest song and accompanying video of successful protesters for Black Lives Matter and other progressive causes, is another corporation that stopped using the moniker "Dixie." Parton has remained mute during this entire ordeal despite never explicitly endorsing the #MeToo movement or any other political rebellion throughout the years. However, a well-known online petition last month demanded that Dolly Parton statues be erected in Tennessee in place of Confederate monuments. (This book actually concludes with a tale about such a monument.)

Many more things have changed since I wrote this. Previously, Dolly Parton's most recent entry into television was an NBC holiday film based on one of her hit songs; currently, it's a Netflix series based on a number of her hit songs. The number of books distributed to children worldwide by Parton's Imagination Library has increased from 80 million to over 133 million since then. Then, I cited another author's excellent claim that performing artist Nicki Minaj shared many traits with Parton; at this point, I'd point out that current pop diva Lizzo exhibits Partonesque traits.

My admiration for Roseanne Barr, whose show character I portrayed as a working-class feminist hero and who subsequently made nasty, racist public comments, has significantly decreased as Dolly's Grammy total has risen.

In recent years, the globe has changed. However, the main ideas and contentions remain. At least one particular aspect also: According to a research released this year, songs performed by female singers still only made up 10% of country radio plays in 2019, which is consistent with the 2016 percentage I cited.

Betty doesn't identify as a feminist, unlike Dolly. She wasn't thinking about the untrue stereotype that second-wave feminists burned their brassieres in protest. She simply had no longer used the items and wanted to watch the straps burn to ash because she planned to wear them comfortably in her retirement years. She may have also had practical and modest reasons for not wanting her underwear to end up in the adjoining hay barn, pig pen, or work shed. Grandma smoked and threw the match, and the Kansas wind started to burn her bras.

It's the sort of stuff that would make a good country song.

Chapter 1:
Embodies the Working Woman's Fight

The Great Smoky Mountains, where Dolly Parton first picked up a guitar, were engulfed in flames as Christmas of Many Colors, her holiday film about struggles and miracles in East Tennessee, made its television debut in November. The death toll would rise to fourteen as the smoke cleared in Parton's hometown of Sevier County. According to Tennessee Governor Bill Haslam, it was the biggest fire to hit the state in a century.

A few hours before the movie premiered, Dolly Parton declared that every family who lost their house will get $1,000 per month for six months from her Dollywood Foundation. For the funding, about 900 households would apply.

A West Virginian friend and filmmaker who focuses on Appalachian poverty made the following comment when I shared the news about Parton's fire victim fund on social media that evening: "My first words after the fires: Dolly will save 'em." 11.5 million viewers were watching Parton's cameo in Christmas of Many Colors as a kind sex worker who was shunned by self-described Christians in her hometown as she composed this.

Auburn-haired "Jolene," the real-life siren Parton claims worked at a bank and flirted with her husband when he came in to transact business, has been the subject of numerous songs; she served as the inspiration for the majority of her original recorded songs. The blond "town tramp" Parton loved as a young girl, however, is the lady to whom music owes a great deal more. Parton modeled her appearance after the woman.

According to Parton, she had "yellow hair piled on top of her head, red lipstick, her eyes all painted up, and her clothes all tight and flashy," as she recalled in a 2016 interview with Southern Living. She was simply the most beautiful creature I had ever seen, in my opinion. That's what I'm going to be when I grow up, I thought when everyone commented, "Oh, she's just trash," Trash!'"

Parton, who is now 71, has retold this tale numerous times since she is a woman whose appearance causes others to ask why. She finally fully honors the "painted lady" in "Christmas of Many Colors" by designating her as the protector angel of a story that is largely based on a Christmas when Parton was a youngster.

In the movie, little Dolly is trying to help her dad and brothers come up with $69.95, plus tax, to finally buy her mom a gold wedding band as she sits on a sidewalk strumming a guitar on a chilly December night as holiday shoppers swarm along the main street of her small hometown. The yellow-haired woman drops a twenty dollar bill into Dolly's guitar bag while wearing tight clothing and high heels, but a self-righteous shopkeeper cleaning the sidewalk forbids the joyous youngster to keep the money contaminated by the woman's misdeeds.

The enraged woman chastises, "You get away from her." Why, this is a divine child. She doesn't want your shady cash. She continues, "Comin' around decent folks all painted up, sticking out everywhere," before sweeping her broom at the woman.

Parton's character responds, "Boy, you and that broom make a good team, you ol' witch," before disappearing into the night and telling little Dolly she's sorry she couldn't give her the money.

This recognizable Parton trifecta—tight clothing that raises eyebrows, generosity of spirit, and a take-no-f**k attitude—

represents an unacknowledged, unidentified form of feminism that I identify in the unfortunate women who nurtured me. They didn't sell their bodies, but they endured ridicule because of their origins. In ninth, tenth, or eleventh grade, the majority of them dropped out. In our lives, there was no feminist philosophy or literature. There was simply life, in which we were women who were economically marginalized, forced to perform sedentary jobs in factories and restaurants, and who were hopelessly sexualized.

When I was a child in the 1980s, my mother drove a UPS truck, dragging and shoving boxes of Christmas presents that she and her own family wouldn't get. Her long red artificial fingernails didn't slow her down. At a department store counter in a Wichita mall, she worked another job applying makeup for middle-class ladies, with a male manager passing by to change the metal name tag attached to her blouse. She was fully aware of what was happening, but she didn't object or voice her complaints—doing so would have put her employment at peril. She understood that the only way a woman without resources or connections could win the game—that is, be able to support herself and her children financially—was by participating in it.

The finest self-aware gender performance in contemporary history and a genuine embodiment of who Parton is, Parton's exaltation of the strengths of this sometimes maligned class of American women in her songwriting, acting roles, and stage presence. She represents the working-class woman who is destitute, whose feminine sexuality is frequently a necessary survival tool, but whose tough presence can be deemed "masculine" in parts of society where women haven't traditionally worked and where the antiquated idea of a "lady" survives. They are unmarried mothers who depend on welfare and need abortions, ladies without degrees but with definite beliefs, and complex individuals who have been reduced in the media to a "backwards" cliché. They have very few ambassadors to represent their grace because they have long been despised as a moral scandal in the US.

What Parton has done for feminism has more to do with her than with feminism, and she is directly responsible for rural poverty. She came by it naturally, as my grandmother used to say about the Appalachian highlands in the middle of the 20th century that alchemized a future tale.

OUTTA THAT HOLLER

Parton, the fourth child of twelve children, was born in 1946 on a modest farm; her father, Lee, gave the doctor a bag of grain in exchange for the delivery. Those who are familiar with her music are aware that wearing feed sack costumes as a child didn't make her miserable; rather, it made her thankful, which ironically helped make her a very wealthy woman. The royalties for her classic 1971 song "Coat of Many Colors," in which she sings of loving a garment her mother made out of trash despite being teased for it at school, keep coming in.

That ode to her mother, Avie Lee, has been cited by Parton as being her most treasured song among her many hits. She attributes her musical ability to that branch of her family, whom she refers to as "dreamers." Radios, record players, and electricity hadn't yet reached the rural poor during Dolly Parton's upbringing, but they passed down traditional European country peasants pastimes to amuse themselves in their own homes. Her paternal grandfather was a Pentecostal minister who also played the violin and composed music.

Billy, the guitarist brother of Avie Lee, heard young Dolly's musical talent. He assisted in getting her a spot on Cas Walker's Farm and Home Hour on radio and television in Knoxville. When Dolly was eight years old, Billy reportedly gave her her first real guitar, an infant-sized acoustic Martin, to replace the one she'd constructed out of an old mandolin and two discarded strings. He assisted her in writing "Puppy Love," her debut single, which she wrote when she was eleven and recorded in 1959 at the age of thirteen following a 30-hour bus voyage with her grandmother to Goldband Records in Lake Charles, Louisiana.

Rock & roll, which had its roots in Southern Black culture, had already swept over white America and infused country music by that point. It was audible in the upbeat dance beat of "Puppy Love" and Uncle Billy's stylish pompadour in the manner of Elvis. The daughter of Alabama sharecroppers, Rose Maddox, was a rockabilly pioneer that Parton revered. But the tunes that really influenced her were the old Appalachian melodies, the inferior European cousins of the African blues of slavery. In one of her early hits, "Apple Jack," she describes meeting a mountain musician who gave her his banjo when he passed away. This banjo was a piece of Africa that had made its way to East Tennessee over the years.

While Parton's mother's family provided her with musical training and guidance, she attributes her business expertise to her father, a kind-hearted lifelong laborer who didn't learn to read or write but was skilled in the horse trade and could make a little money go a long way. Her father's emphasis on their modest home had a significant impact on the bright business mind that later created an empire with a value in the hundreds of millions of dollars.

During her 2016 tour in support of her most recent album, Pure and Simple, she spoke about those seemingly incompatible interests— "getting out" and being where you most belong—on stage in Kansas City. With only three backup musicians and a few white fabric cascades, Parton performed in that show without the elaborate sets and backup bands that were a staple of so many of her tours. The performance began with the sound of crickets and the flash of lightning-like lamps.

During the performance, Parton ascended a few steps to sit on what was initially thought to be a front porch but turned out to be an elevated platform for communicating with the afterlife. She paid homage to her father's laborious work, wise financial judgments, and dedication to his family before singing "Smoky Mountain Memories," her 1978 song about poor laborers drawn north during the mid-century factory boom.

She recalled people begging her dad to "go up hair, get them kids outta that holler." But when Dolly was a young toddler, after a brief stay in Detroit, Lee declared he would pass away in the East Tennessee mountains. He was aware that although they wouldn't have much there, they would have food and shelter and would be at home.

To start the number, Parton got up and played her flute. She claimed that she was unable to sit during the performance because her father deserved a standing ovation. Thousands of people instantly stood up—her audiences would perform the Hokey Pokey if she requested it—and Parton chuckled.

She exclaimed, "Not from you!" as the audience joined her in laughing. After that, they sat as she sang and sobbed.

Turning to Avie Lee, Parton introduced "Coat of Many Colors" with parallel stories of her mother's inventiveness in the face of hardship. Parton described how Avie would send the kids outdoors to choose the best rock so she could cook "stone soup" to cheer them up. Avie always had the intention of choosing and praising the child who had the roughest day.

One could speculate that Parton, who informed the audience her family had running water "if we ran and got it," received her wit and innate poetic ability from her mother's speech. Parton recalled her mother to the audience, "If we had some ham, we'd have ham and eggs—if we had some eggs."

Considering that she spent eighteen years in her parents' cabin as opposed to more than 50 years in Nashville and elsewhere, the majority of which she spent at the height of her fame and money, Parton has been reiterating these anecdotes for decades. But despite having heard it a thousand times before, fans nevertheless stand in line to hear it again, perhaps because there are so few celebrities who can claim to actually own such experiences. That ownership is evident in its humor.

Women in underprivileged areas prefer to joke about poverty, whereas those from more fortunate backgrounds seem to view it with profound sadness—perhaps as a sign of their own guilt or ignorance of what makes people happy. A tale that is more complicated than a melancholy lament can be told thanks to first-hand experience. Because they never had to pretend to be moved by gifts that their husbands couldn't buy, those women developed a dry sense of humor as a result of the disconnect between their reality and the middle-class ideals depicted in magazine advertisements.

For instance, my grandma told her the story of my biological grandfather proposing to her when she was sixteen and became pregnant with my mother, and she did it with a cigarette drag.

It wasn't anything like, 'Please be my beloved wife.' Sheeeeit," she replied, and we both laughed—not at the miseries of our own families, but rather at the illusions of women who received emotional proposals and large diamond engagement rings before spending their entire lives pushing a vacuum.

If Parton's music doesn't have that edge, you haven't really listened to much of it. Her early songs, in particular, frequently reference angry, hypocritical, and even deadly males, women who are mistreated and degraded, and dying infants. (The infant sister Parton was tasked with taking care of was ill and passed away.) Parton is well known for her "fake" appearance, which includes wigs, synthetic clothing that clings to a body that has had surgery, and pastel-colored acrylic nails. However, when she writes, Parton can be a very dark realist. The divine feminine of American roots music can be heard in the depths of a woman's voice and the straightforward tales of hell on earth that are sung by women who have only their faith to keep them going.

Her 2001 album "Little Sparrow," which blends bluegrass, folk, and country gospel sounds from her native country, features the song "Little Sparrow," which is sung in the voice of a betrayed, saddened woman admonishing young girls to "never trust the hearts of men." As eerie as the melody is, Parton introduces it with a jest on stage: "I call it my little sad-ass song." Parton is prone to undercut solemn times with a charming bit of nervous humor.

According to Parton, it is impossible to be from her hometown and not enjoy dreadful music. The scariest tales she crafts about those mountains in her music appear to be based on what she observed in front of her family's home. Her father's refusal to say "I love you"—a widespread cultural illness for males of all classes in that era and, possibly to a lesser extent, still today—is the largest complaint she has raised about her childhood. However, Parton believes that in reality, her family's love was so abundant that every material need was met.

At a different stop on the same tour, in Austin, Texas, Parton made her way down the steps of the "porch" before it was rolled offstage following the touching tribute to her musical mother and hardworking father.

She pronounced, "Time to come down from heaven, I reckon," and a strong, bare-armed man wearing a black vest and hat who had been presented as her "sexy cowboy" performed a new instrument. She was now playing the flute, dulcimer, and guitar. Like all of her other instruments, including the grand piano she played for one song, it was white and coated in rhinestones.

Parton remarked, "Oh, the cowboy brought me a banjo." Soon she was playing "Rocky Top," a bluegrass tune that praises the Tennessee hills, on it with her talon fingernails. Just a few miles from Parton's hometown of Gatlinburg, which was the area most severely affected by the current wildfires, the song was penned in 1967 by a married couple of innkeepers.

Parton handed her a fiddle while the cowboy threw the banjo over her back for the bridge. Parton tapped the air with her bow like a conductor while the quick beat pulsated and another member of her band played a banjo. She aimed the blow towards the cowboy just before she began her solo, saying in time to the beat, "You dance." She fiddled, the crowd yelled, and the handsome cowboy kicked up his heels while hooking his thumbs into the belt loops of his tight trousers.

Parton takes more time than the normal performer bowing down to others onstage while displaying what appears to be genuine humility. She acknowledges the audience, thanks her band, and pays tribute to her heritage and family. However, it was Parton's own joy, wants, and power that were on display at that point in the performance, with faces still damp from the emotional songs for mama and daddy. The hot piece of man sitting next to her was on her payroll, and she sang the song and performed two instruments on it. He danced when she said "dance."

In her 1994 autobiography, My Life and Other Unfinished Business, Dolly Parton claimed that sex was the third major influence on her life after music and religion. She used to visit an abandoned chapel as a child that had shattered windows, warped flooring, and condom wrappers left underneath the porch by teens. The chapel also had a broken piano and "dirty drawings" on the walls. Parton claimed that in that environment of music, sex, and God, she had a spiritual realization that "it was all right for me to be a sexual being." She has acknowledged that she was both internally and externally precocious in terms of hormones.

Her shape was famously nipped, tucked, and elevated throughout the years, but it was just as unbelievable as if it had grown organically. She became aware of her own sexual power early on because of the male attention it attracted. Lacking lipstick, she dyed her lips with iodine from the medicine cabinet. The rigid patriarchal religion of her people saw this desire for erotic behavior as disrespectful to her parents.

She spoke about her father disciplining her for making herself up in a 2003 Rolling Stone interview. She recalled admonishing, "'This is my natural color!'" "It got redder the more Daddy attempted to rub it off. 'This red ass of yours after a whipping, is that your natural color?' Oh, I'm really pissed off about makeup.

Both her mother and her preacher grandfather trembled, fearing that the devil had guided Dolly in Jezebel's direction. In her 1983 television program Dolly in London, Parton referred to herself as "the original punk rocker." She pierced her own ears in the early 1960s as a teenager so she could hang feathers from them and rattail her hair. Parton advised her mother to give credit where credit is due—not to Satan but to Dolly herself—when she indicated that she had been possessed.

She recalled in her autobiography, "I couldn't make my hair big enough or 'yaller' enough, couldn't get my skirt tight enough, couldn't get my blouses low enough. "... Of course, I needed to leave the house to actually work the dog. I used to take shots by unbuttoning my blouse, raising my headlights with my arms, and entering Woolworth's four-for-a-quarter photo booth.

Women who didn't grow up on a farm may not realize that in the region where Parton was from, this typical gesture of female adolescent disobedience wasn't merely intended to appeal to boys. It was about asserting her femininity in a setting where both men and women had to draw on "masculine" qualities and minimize their "feminine" counterparts in order to thrive.

"My sisters and I used to cling desperately to anything halfway feminine," wrote Parton. The newspapers that lined the walls of our home and the sporadic glances we caught at magazines both had images of the models. We desired to resemble them. They did not appear to be required to work in the fields in any way. They didn't appear as though they needed to take a dishpan spit bath.

For Parton, store-bought clothing and lipstick symbolized a level of economic agency that might shield a woman from attack as well as a life beyond laborious manual labor. In fact, studies show that women who are poor are more likely to experience serious male violence.

In those hills, "womanhood was a difficult thing to get a hold of, unless you were a man," Parton penned. "[Glamourous ladies in magazines] didn't look like they were open to having their hands touched whenever and as roughly they wanted. Given how they seemed, any man who wanted to touch them had better be pretty polite.

Male violence affects women from all social classes. But there is a harsh reality to Parton's perspective. She had white skin, good health, and a ton of talent on her side for the upcoming social ascent. A poor person, however, is something that the world values even less than a girl.

Even though my family's poverty was minimal compared to Parton's, it was enough for me to feel embarrassed. Since we lived in a rural area of Kansas, I didn't experience it until I attended school, where I could compare and contrast the attire and lives of other kids with my own.

On the first day, the reckoning started even before I arrived at the school: I boarded the bus as it approached our long dirt road carrying a paper grocery bag full of goods. I had been blissfully unaware as my mother, armed with a little calculator and her plastic coupon organizer, checked items off of the teacher's supplied list. However, I was the only student on the bus whose supplies weren't in a backpack, and by the time we arrived at the school—nearly an hour after all the required stops, snaking around dirt roads and ruts—I felt ashamed when I unloaded the brand-new crayons and pencils I had carefully selected from a paper sack.

You have two options in such circumstances if you are a non-tantrum-throwing youngster like I was: drop your head and cry, or tilt your chin forward and let the tears inside of you transform into a salty form of power. The ladies I knew had taught me the latter ability, which is a special strength for a woman because she will be required to take care of others in addition to herself throughout her life. Such a life leaves little room for one's own grievances.

All musical genres and, in fact, all forms of art have the trait of transforming suffering into power. But for women living in poverty, it is more than simply a song; it is a way of life, a requirement.

Parton's music conveys this, just as that of Loretta Lynn, Tammy Wynette, Patsy Cline, and numerous other female country musicians before and after.

Her unique twist, in contrast to most of the others, is that she transmits it with palpable optimism and a grin. She profoundly understands the relationship between a challenging past and a fortunate present. Her goal in life and on stage is to respect that tension in other people's lives.

No matter where they are from, she tells her audiences that no one deserves to be shamed, and that everyone can relate to it in some way. She exhorts the cheering masses, "Never be ashamed of your home, your family, yourself, or your religion." One need only consider Dolly Parton's enormous LGBTQ fan base to see that her journey from a gifted but slut-shamed young bumpkin to an entertainment superstar reflects a universal struggle that has less to do with being Appalachian than it does with being human. If her presence and the gratitude it inspires in others could be summed up in one word, it would be "be what you are."

However, Parton would have to be the person who left behind both poverty and place in order to spread that message to the whole public—in order to share the stories of the poor ladies from the area where she was born. Although doing so required her to say goodbye to her closest friends and family, she didn't have a hard time making the choice.

She wrote in her autobiography about attending a traveling circus as a young girl and being shocked to see her cousin Myrtle dressed as the "alligator girl."

Parton remarked, "I could understand her perfectly. After all, I desired attention and desired to flee the mountains. I didn't mean to embarrass her or expose her, but I just wanted to say hello and "Hello, I get it." Act like an alligator. Be whatever your goals and good fortune will allow you to be.

Of course, Parton had musical fantasies. She played with chickens while also practicing her guitar and putting an empty tin can on a stick placed in between the porch boards of her family's home. Her aspirations, however, also included fame. In light of this, it doesn't matter how talented you are if you're only performing for yourself on your front porch.

Fortunately, Uncle Billy drove an automobile. He had to crawl in and out of the passenger side since the driver's side door was wired to stay on the frame while the car was in motion. Over the years, he would take Parton to Nashville, some 200 miles to the east, to knock on doors. After being rejected by record executives, they spent the night in his car and drove back to the farm in Sevier County the next morning.

TALKING THROUGH SONGS

A few years ago, Parton honored Bill Owens with an area filled with pictures and memorabilia at Dollywood, the theme park she established in her hometown in 1986. Parton sings a song to her uncle Billy from a small screen in a video that many of the park's 3 million annual visitors watch.

In the song, she remembers the two of them daydreaming about a world beyond those hills when duties were finished, and his instructions on how to select, yodel, overcome her worries, and conduct appropriately in public. She sings, "You told me I was special, and I took it to heart. She repeatedly says the words "I love you" in the chorus, which Billy may have found difficult to pronounce because his father was unable to do it.

But Parton is today the most successful female performer in the annals of country music, in large part thanks to the patient guidance of that Tennessee man. She is a member of the Songwriters Hall of Fame and has sold well over 100 million CDs. Since 1964, she has published more than three thousand songs, ranging from gospel to country to pop. She is one of the six female winners of the Country Music Association's entertainer of the year award. Following two well-received TV movies, a series following her early years is apparently in development.

Parton's forty-third solo album, Pure and Simple, debuted at number one on the Billboard country album chart in August 2016 after more than fifty years in the industry—her first time in that position in twenty-five years.

Since Nashville's sound dramatically shifted away from twang in the early 1990s, her work has received almost no radio airplay. The fact that it was her biggest North American tour in 25 years, stopping in more than 60 locations, didn't stop her admirers from filling the venues.

Grandma Betty, who I surprised with tickets to see Dolly Parton's tour in Kansas City last summer, had never attended a large-arena performance before she turned age 71 (she and Parton were born eight months apart). As previously said, our family does not have money to spare for expensive event tickets. For the occasion, I had pictured us donning similar shirts and pouring Aqua Net onto matching beehives, but the trip and everything it symbolized to us— for instance, that we weren't as poor as we formerly were—was overwhelming enough.

Betty and Dolly are the same age, but they also come from slightly comparable backgrounds. Both of them had an outhouse in their homes—Betty's was temporary but nevertheless served as a stark class distinction for people of her generation. Both of them detested going to school and felt excluded there. When she was a fourteen-year-old waitress in Wichita on St. Patrick's Day, Betty colored her hair green; when the scandalized supervisor told her to go home, she refused to go so she could rinse the color out of her hair. Betty was punk before punk was hip. Betty was a highly attractive young lady in the 1960s and 1970s when she wore huge, blond wigs and miniskirts.

Betty's family had a car, a small house instead of a cabin, and there were four kids instead of twelve, so they fared a little better financially than Dolly. In the parents category, she was dealt a much worse hand than Dolly. Her mother, a restaurant chef and occasionally factory worker, had untreated mental illness; her father, a violent drinker who was raised on a farm west of Wichita, was a factory worker. That could be the reason Betty went on to experience personally the things Dolly, it seems, merely observed and sang about in songs: adolescent pregnancies, single motherhood, violent marriages, and adult poverty.

Betty used to put one of Dolly's recordings in the car's deck when I was a kid while we drove along a highway. In that emotionally constrained Midwestern culture and class, that is the only music I can recall her singing and crying to.

Grandma Betty, whose farmhouse I moved into permanently when I was eleven years old and who was only thirty-four when she found out she'd be my grandmother, and I watched the concert in Kansas City together, and it was like watching two women's lives that had somewhat similar beginnings but very different outcomes share the same space. Betty's reactions caught my attention more than my own, which is a habit anyone from a troubled household might have because observation serves as a way to both distance oneself from bad situations and keep an eye out for disaster. (People frequently enquire as to how I, as a writer, can recall so much from my early years, and I believe Parton's response may be similar—if I wanted a different kind of existence, I had to pay close attention to the choices and circumstances of those around me.)

But I laughed a lot throughout the concert.
When Parton added, "People ask me what it was like to work with Burt Reynolds," it was clear from her tone that it would be much more appropriate to ask Reynolds about her experience. Well, my favorite movie experiences involved ladies. The audience cheered enthusiastically when Steel Magnolias and 9 to 5 were mentioned.

Parton added, "Open the dang door," as an afterthought, following the final note of her new song "Outside Your Door," in which a lustful woman knocks somewhere she apparently shouldn't be. You're certain you want it. The audience cheered and laughed.

Unspoken for a moment, a man yelled, "I LOVE YOU DOLLYYYYYY!"

She retaliated, "I thought I told you to wait in the truck," with a quick remark. The audience laughed and applauded despite the fact that she has used that statement at every performance since the Lyndon B. Johnson administration.

She claimed that she had fired her drummer because he had become inebriated, but it didn't matter because the keyboard's drum machine had saved her thousands of dollars. Again, the audience laughed and applauded.

Before beginning that timeless song, she remarked, "Jolene could have worked at a bank, but I went to the bank many times with this little song I penned. On that one, the crowd roared with laughter and physically trembled with enthusiasm.

Betty laughed along the way too, but not in the same way that she used to. She hasn't had to pay for expensive doctors to keep her healthy over the years, unlike Parton, and in our cramped seats halfway up the vast arena, her knees were hurting.

A woman who lived the song would not feel as happy, but I managed to convince her to stand up and dance with me during "9 to 5," for which the entire venue was on its feet near the end of the show.

Betty began working as a secretary at the county courthouse in downtown Wichita in the 1970s. She then served as one of the city's first female police officers in the reserves before becoming a bailiff, subpoena officer, and probation officer for the criminal courts. She accomplished all of this while attracting a lot of male attention, including, in that professional setting, the same male attorneys who, in theory, would defend her in a sexual harassment complaint. It couldn't have been simple.

It took me some time to realize that the performance was a very significant event for me, too. I was worried about Betty's enjoyment because I knew she was craving a smoke. I had only attended one other mega-concert in my lifetime, despite the fact that I had grown up to be an avid fan of live music, closely following alt-country groups, and helping my then-husband, a professional guitarist, load in and out of bars for years. In the late 1980s, over 30 years ago, my dad, a carpenter for whom such a performance was also a rarity, surprised me by taking me to watch Reba McEntire perform at the Kansas State Fair.

Dad recently admitted to me with considerable sorrow that he likely drank a few beers and a whiskey before we left our rural road and traveled on the flat highway to the fairgrounds. When we arrived, McEntire was hardly visible from our bleacher seat due to the venue's sequins and glitter. I sang along with every song, but it was such a significant event for us that Dad used our 110-mm film camera to take shots of the stage to document our presence.

If there had ever been any kids' tees available, retail vendors were out of them after the show. The only item they had available was a pink adult-sized T-shirt with a shattered heart and the lyrics to one of McEntire's biggest singles at the time, "What Am I Gonna Do About You," which Dad stood in line to purchase for me.

Dad's car wouldn't start when we walked out into the packed parking lot late at night. Until he started the engine with assistance from a stranger, headlights rushed past us. On the lengthy drive home through the pitch-black countryside, I used my enormous new T-shirt as a blanket while I slept next to Dad. For the following two years, I used it as a nightgown.

The most touching part of that memory for me is how my dad, a country boy and the youngest of six children raised on a farm just down the road from the house he built for us out of money he saved from a small concrete-pouring business he ran for a few years, went to the concert for his daughter despite not being a fan of country music.

The question is, "How do you listen to that stuff?" He used to say when I needed nudges to get out of bed to catch the school bus and my alarm clock was blasting 1980s pop-country in the early morning. It is very sad.

Country music was the primary language of ladies in my family. It's how we communicated with one another in a setting where emotions weren't talked about.

When Mom would remark, "Listen to the words," a song would play on her record player, eight-track player, or tape deck and would have a message about life, about men, or about survival. Wynonna and Naomi Judd, K. T. Oslin, Janie Fricke, Lorrie Morgan, Anne Murray, and of course Dolly, Tammy, Patsy, and Loretta all contributed their vocal talents. But because she was listening to those songs personally and I was present to hear them, my mother passed down the information to me. The song "Little Rock" by Reba, which isn't about an Arkansas town but rather about taking a ring off one's finger, was playing frequently in our living room just before my mom and dad got divorced.

One of my biggest advantages is being able to trace my upbringing against a soundtrack of declarative songs sung by women with big hair and denim outfits. We weren't a musical family, but my mother and grandmother, who raised me, cared deeply about music because it helped to validate the tales of our lives as working-class women, spouses, and mothers in a way that TV shows, movies, books, magazines, and newspapers hardly ever did.

Living in the country meant regular trips "to town" to buy this or that or, say, to work at the Wichita mall for the holidays as my mom occasionally did for extra money in the 1980s while little prairie communities surrounding us were disappearing due to economic degradation. That led to a lot of time spent on the roadway. Mom and I avoided eye contact and sang the same lyrics together while listening to country music—usually performed by women—as it rolled down the flat Kansas countryside. Mom grabbed the wheel and tapped the air with one of her long, red fingernails while smoke from her cigarette streamed out of the cracked window.

One song we wore out on a tape together, "Letter Home," by the Forester Sisters from their 1988 album Sincerely, is about women interacting with each other covertly. The lyrics are written by a twenty-nine-year-old woman who is writing to her mother to inform her that her husband has left her for another woman and that their marriage is gone. My mother, though for different circumstances, became a newly divorced young woman a year after that song was released.

"Letter Home" started playing one day while I was an adult sitting in my mother's living room. We were ecstatic to discover that we both recalled every phrase. I was the young woman who had just gotten divorced at the time.

With regard to this line in particular, Mom fell silent and listened as if she were hearing it for the first time as the mother: "He said he felt like a man with her, and I watched them drive away / Children and rent—there was no time for tears, just time to carry on."

Mom suddenly spoke, shocked. She questioned, "He said 'felt like a man with her, and I watched them drive away'?" How do you feel about having that boot up your arse?

We were doubled over with laughter. Neither of us felt the need to explain that every woman we knew, including ourselves, had only ever left, never been left.

But after the second verse, which mentioned the women the narrator works with, Mom stopped laughing. She was particularly moved by the phrase, "We raise our kids and our jeans still fit / and sometimes we go out at night."

Mom replied softly, "Our jeans still fit," and she regarded the horizon. "Yep." She slowly nodded, losing her smile as one eyebrow was raised in recognition.

She was aware that a working-class woman's body form greatly influences her chances of surviving. Not so much because she wants to "catch a man"—the guys she has the opportunity to meet are broke, too, and don't think she doesn't know it—but more because one of the few abilities she possesses is understanding the value of the female form as an object in society. Her body is hers, unlike pricey college degrees and prestigious material things, and how it appears will determine the financial trajectory of her life: Whether she has a good enough appearance to land a position at the makeup counter. Whether the UPS manager, who scowls that she's too little for the job, can be persuaded in the interview with a grin. whether the risky loan will be approved by the banker.

(As it happens, Rush Limbaugh cynically paired up his talk show's periodic "feminist update," which frequently criticizes women for their appearance, with the Forester Sisters' 1991 song "Men," which playfully presents a gloomy picture of the male gender.)

Even beyond these sexual overtones, the working-class woman faces physical risks related to a simple matter of respect. Poor women are mocked in popular culture for being obese, having horrible teeth, and dressing poorly. Every encounter a woman has during the day is influenced by all those class-symbolizing indicators of health and looks. Each of those exchanges determines the survival of the woman who has no money in the bank.

Dolly Parton is one woman who, of course, comprehends this.
Discussions on Parton's musical brilliance should go much beyond and above issues of class and gender. However, the songs she penned will always be associated with the person who sung them, just as her popularity will always be linked to having modeled her appearance after the "town trollop" of her native holler. She gained a reputation tinged with mockery as a result; during interviews with Barbara Walters and Oprah Winfrey in the 1970s and 1980s, both women

urged her to stand up so they could make the unfunny observation that she resembled a tramp.

Johnny Cash is renowned for wearing black as a sign of defiance against the established status quo and on behalf of the oppressed, and he received praise for it. But that's the distinction between being a man and a woman making a deliberate fashion statement.

The women who lack a voice, a platform, or a college education are the ones who truly comprehend what Parton has been up to for fifty years. Dolly Parton's music, movie roles, and persona have impacted the lives of economically disenfranchised women who are accustomed to being shamed or victimized. This may be another source of affection between Parton and some segments of her fanbase that hundreds, if not thousands, of interviews have failed to reveal.

There are several valid responses to that query, but one of them is this: At the age of seventy, Dolly Parton made a Christmas movie and cast herself in the lead part as a shooed-away sex worker who later returns to aid a young girl.

It is well known that Parton never forgot her roots or abandoned her community, whose economy now depends on her tourist attractions, whose children benefit from the books and scholarships her foundation offers, and who's recently burned-out homes will be rebuilt with her assistance. Less has been stated about the degree to which she continued to identify with a certain American woman archetype, the one whose trailer makes the rest of the world label her "trash." She may not be white, but she undoubtedly is poor, and she most certainly did not have the opportunity to study feminism in a college classroom.

Years ago, Parton might have improved her appearance by performing songs that didn't belong on the Cracker Barrel CD rack, using less makeup like ladies who can afford it, or both. Instead, she developed her persona and created her songs in such a way that she is unable to sing or look in the mirror without speaking for the daily unheard and unvalidated women. The music contains the conversation between Parton and those women. They are somewhere cleaning the mirrors in the toilets of truck stops and diners while listening to country music.

THE GREAT UNIFIER

Before Grandma Betty and I went to see Dolly Parton perform in June, I was browsing Twitter one evening and noticed that Parton kept popping up in my account. It had been two days after the United Kingdom's stunning referendum to leave the European Union, which had profound cultural and economic repercussions. "Is 'Brexit' the Precursor to a Donald Trump Presidency?" read one headline in the New York Times. (The column, incidentally, provided the wrong solution to the question.) In a gay nightclub in Orlando, Florida, a shooter had slain 49 people a few weeks earlier. Democrats had just stormed the House floor in Washington, DC, to perform a sit-in in support of passing gun control legislation.

However, Parton with a little bejeweled saxophone appeared among the dark political tweet cloud on my computer screen. A few tweets later, she was back, this time appearing in a video where she and her small band were singing 1960s protest songs a cappella. Twice more political tweets, then Parton. I discovered that some of my New York City pals had attended her performance in Queens.

She recently began her Pure and Simple tour, which I was completely unaware of. I didn't understand why so many New Yorkers seemed to know more about Dolly than I did.

The gang behind the Dolly tweets that were coming in from New York contacts cut over racial, ethnic, religious, and sexual boundaries. But they were all female.

One user tweeted, "That majestic bitch just started playing a goddamn PANFLUTE [sic],"

Another person added, "Dolly Parton, sitting in a pew onstage, just got a stadium full of Nyers to shout "Amen." Then it was stated that "nothing says #Pride like a stadium full of gays singing 'Here You Come Again' with Dolly Parton."

Two New York acquaintances who I had no idea were acquainted at the time started tweeting back and forth.

Her voice is flawless.
"Dolly always! Who knew she could tell such good tales?
I'm about to leap onto the stage.

I was then entertained, moved, and a little taken aback, having never previously been a member of Parton's live audiences. When I spent a few years living in New York, I organized a party with the sole objective of teaching people how to line dance and sending them home with CD mixes of music other than hipster-approved David Allen Coe because I've been criticized about country music so many times. I think I assumed that Dolly Parton would only be ironically adored in certain communities.

I knew Parton was a global phenomenon, of course, but I didn't understand how much non-"country" people adored her—not just as a "crossover" musician but also as the down-to-earth, even religious persona she portrayed on her most recent tour. The fact that she consistently sings about poverty and rural existence while wearing a wig and embellishments is perhaps what makes her so endearing to those from circumstances that are utterly dissimilar to her own.

One aspect of Parton's attractiveness is that I feel a connection to her and her songs as a fellow country working-class woman. Numerous celebrities draw sizable crowds, but Parton's work and persona foster a connection among seemingly unrelated people.

During the tour last year, Dolly drag queens turned to the crowds and ordered large groups to move to the music. People who seemed to be swayed included wrinkled people wearing Wrangler jeans, pierced teenagers wearing all black, big men wearing T-shirts that said "proud redneck," gay men who knew the words to every song, kids who knew the same words, lesbian couples holding hands, college students holding a beer in both hands, seen-it-all women like my grandma Betty, and most everyone in between.

Being among them allows one to witness and experience the strength of a lady who actually embodies Jesus' teachings to "love your enemies and do not judge" in contrast to the hollow Christianity that so much of Nashville's country music industry erroneously propagates. It is an energy that is impossible to mimic. Everyone in the room senses it, and Parton expresses her recognition of it.

She urged the Austin audience in December, "Wouldn't it be nice if we could take a little vial of this love energy out there?" In America, on the verge of what was certain to be another difficult year, people cheered and sobbed.

Parton usually never engages in politics, but she received flak last year for her stance on the presidential election from both sides of the party divide. Parton had a positive response when the New York Times asked her what she felt about a woman running for president.

She claimed that Hillary Clinton might be the best president to ever have served. "... In my opinion, a woman would do a fantastic job. Hillary is quite qualified, in my opinion. So if she succeeds, she has my full support.

Several of her conservative fans swore on blogs and social media that they would never purchase her music or concert tickets again. In a statement that she released later, Parton clarified that "if she gets it" was referring to the president rather than the Democratic nomination, which wasn't yet final.

"My comment about supporting a woman in the White House was taken out of context," the statement said. In later interviews, she claimed that she hadn't even made up her mind and that she hadn't endorsed any candidate.

Then, when Donald Trump was the Republican nominee, the left erupted in rage at the notion that Hillary would even consider supporting him. They would also never purchase her CDs or concert tickets in the future.

Of course, the vast majority will continue to purchase. Not only does Parton bridge racial and ethnic divides, but she also bridges the awful political split of today.

Parton incorporated her trademark puns and self-deprecating humor into her 2016 concert tour, saying that regardless of who won the election—Clinton or Trump—the nation would experience "PMS" or "presidential mood swings." She avoids politics, but if she were to run, she would have the right hair—it's huge, she remarked, mimicking Trump. Perhaps they didn't need any more "boobs" in the race after all.

Although Parton has frequently risked her sales in the same political climate that resulted in the Dixie Chicks being shunned by Nashville and country radio when they criticized then-President George W. Bush following the 2003 invasion of Iraq, such crowd-pleasing diplomacy may have something to do with business.

For instance, in 2006, after decades of outspoken advocacy on behalf of the LGBTQ community, she penned the song "Travelin' Thru" for the Transamerica soundtrack. The song, which she played at the Academy Awards when it was a best song nomination, has references to roots songs about arduous, transformational travels, such as the folk song "Wayfaring Stranger" from the nineteenth century and the early twentieth-century country gospel classic "I Am a Pilgrim." The song's soundtrack number incorporates that history while honoring the challenges of transgender persons on a personal, societal, and political level. We've all been crucified, and they nailed Jesus to the tree, and when I'm born again, you're going to notice a change in me, Parton sings in their voice.

As a result of her involvement in the film, Parton allegedly received death threats. She has stated that as a cisgender, heterosexual woman whose look is regarded as weird and whose sex life has been probed, she empathizes with individuals who are derided or labeled "freaks" for their experiences of sexuality or gender. Years ago, there were persistent rumors that she had a lesbian connection with a childhood acquaintance who frequently accompanied her. She asserts that if that were the case, she would come out with pride; she has been married to the same man for fifty years; he was a Tennessean who worked in the concrete industry. She claims that rather than her own sexuality, her nonjudgmental acceptance of theirs is what her LGBTQ fans find appealing.

Parton's dislike of overtly political speech may have a lot to do with her upbringing. Even though they are interested in politics, many members of my family avoid discussing it because they lack the time or the specialized language needed to interact with the chattering class.

I have three college degrees and work as a professional communicator, but even I have been chastised for using the incorrect term or structure on Twitter. My perspective wasn't systemic enough, or the phrase I used wasn't widely used in academic jargon. Imagine you lived in a rural location before the internet, like Parton and the women in my family, and you hadn't attended school since you were a teenager. No matter how worldly you become, if that is your background, formal, scholarly talk is going to intimidate you or at the very least make you uncomfortable. See Dolly Parton's 2009 commencement speech at the University of Tennessee, in which she confesses that despite the many stages she has ruled, she still feels anxious speaking in front of a packed auditorium of graduates wearing caps and gowns. She says it with trembling, which is strange to see in a lady whose tremendous confidence has long been on display in public.

Whatever the motivations behind Parton's preference for telling personal tales over political arguments, the world's current state of unrest couldn't be more appropriate for that propensity. In the weeks leading up to the 2016 presidential election, a number of my friends—White, Black, and Latina, with diverse class backgrounds among them—commented that Dolly Parton was a sort of slave, a spiritual leader when political leaders are failing.

Like any great storyteller, her politics are lived directly rather than discussed in academic jargon, evaluated as experience rather than as abstract concepts, and occur at the human level. Both the didactic argument and the self-contained narrative have their place. Parton is involved in the first.

She didn't make a political tweet about race or immigration last year; instead, she pledged through her organization to assist every Tennessee wildfire victim. According to Jeff Conyers, executive director of the Dollywood Foundation, the group was worried that immigrants without a legal status wouldn't seek assistance. In order to communicate their lack of "out to catch" intentions across linguistic hurdles, the foundation sought out influential members of the Hispanic community. In order to connect people with relief funding, no inquiries or records of citizenship, race, or ethnicity were made. In a similar spirit, beneficiaries were trusted with the assistance funds and were not compelled to provide reports or follow-ups.

As a result of the wildfires, I am reminded of my West Virginian friend's remark that "Dolly will save 'em."

She seems to be able to achieve this in part because her lifetime of displaying love while avoiding doctrine encourages others to do good deeds. She and her organization organized a traditional telethon in December of last year that was also live streamed online in order to generate money for the fire victims. Within a few hours, they had amassed $9 million. When Parton phoned, everyone from pop icon Cyndi Lauper to rising musician Chris Stapleton performed. While Parton was speaking with Billy Ray Cyrus, Paul Simon called in with a $100,000 donation.

Parton has pals all throughout the world. A man who claimed to be homeless approached me as I was penning this story in a coffee shop in Wichita and inquired as to what I was writing about. When I told him, he became enthused and regaled me with Parton's life story, concluding with praise for the authenticity of her voice in a time when so much music is produced using computer manipulation.

He remarked, "She doesn't need any of that. "Her pipes are her pipes, no matter how many years go by or how she looks."

Parton's popularity began to soar the same year as everything in America seemed to be going south, so perhaps this is no coincidence. Dolly Parton is one lady who simultaneously embodies the past and present, rich and poor, feminine and masculine, Jezebel and Holy Mother, the adventure of getting out and the beautiful return to home. A shattered thing needs completeness, and that's what Dolly Parton delivers.

This is just everything, to paraphrase a friend of mine from New York City who was live-tweeting Dolly Parton's concert in June.

THE LAST LAUGH

Parton quips that she had to become wealthy in order to resume singing in a terrible voice.
She was the same spirit inside a talented poor girl in that holler in the middle of the 20th century. She possessed a guitar, a supportive uncle, and a loving family, but she yearned to disappear somewhere where she would be seen. According to Parton, she was the subject of harsh rumors about the kind of girl she was in high school. She claims that she was unable to escape before becoming eighteen because she believed her father would send a posse after her.

Every student in the class was asked to come up and discuss their plans when she graduated from Sevier County High School in 1964, becoming the first member of her family to receive a diploma. She informed her classmates that she was moving to Nashville to become a celebrity, as she would recall in her University of Tennessee graduation speech. They laughed out loud.

She gave her family a final hug the following morning before heading to the bus stop.

Her life, as well as the world, was about to undergo a significant upheaval while she waited for the bus. The Civil Rights Act would become a law in a matter of weeks. The quest for equal rights has sparked the largest women's movement since that time. However, Parton's experience in East Tennessee would serve as the inspiration for many of her songs, as well as a manual for how to properly interact with the guys in suits in Nashville and a call to generosity toward those in need.

Parton was unaware of everything. All she knew was that she was relocating to a sizable, unfamiliar location to carry out a task for which she had been preparing for years. She had all of her possessions in her hands. She carried a deeper sense of self-worth and an unflinching sense of humor about the challenges she had faced along the road.

She set up a joke she has frequently recounted in her memoirs when she said, "I boarded a Greyhound bus with my dreams, my old guitar, the songs I had written, and the rest of my belongings in a set of matching luggage—three paper bags from the same grocery store."

Chapter 2:
Masters the Art of Leaving

Dolly Parton was questioned by Billboard magazine in 2014 regarding feminism. The interviewer asked, "Are you familiar with Sheryl Sandberg's book Lean In?"
The question "What is it?" Parton enquired.
The interviewer said, "Lean In—it's a book." The question is, "Have you ever 'leaned in'?"

Parton laughed and remarked, "I've leaned over," possibly innuendo. "I'm bending forward. I have no idea what 'leaned in' means.

This might explain Dolly Parton's roots: a place where a woman's strength and independence are more about walking than talking. Parton is a legendary female trailblazer in music, business, and popular culture. Social progression in the women's movement has depended heavily on this talk—the articulation, research, and theories of progress toward gender parity. What poor and working-class women do to the cause, however, is equally important but receives less recognition.

Their worlds frequently rebel against the box of politicized language, which is typically the domain of people with college educations. But "uneducated" women have witnessed the most horrific effects of gender inequality: starving mothers with hungry kids; abusive wives who live in remote areas and are too poor to access the judicial system; and underpaid, dangerous employment that makes the fingers bleed. For these women, the struggle for survival alone is a claim to equality that may be referred to as "feminist." But here's the thing: In my experience, it doesn't matter what you label it, right or wrong.

The Women's March and associated walkout on International Women's Day earlier this year once again highlighted the long-standing socioeconomic divide that frequently runs across political movements. Today's vital political resistance owes a lot to the toil and rage of civically active women, especially with the Oval Office being held by an admitted sexual predator. The ability to engage in such activity, however, is greatly influenced by economic agency. You can bet that the majority of images of protesters sporting pink "pussy" hats show middle- or upper-class women who can take time off from work, get a ride to the protest venue, or pay for a babysitter.

Marches and strikes are something to simultaneously applaud and view with some suspicion for a woman like myself, a feminist who grew up in a location that was more like Dolly Parton's childhood home in rural Tennessee than like a well-connected progressive hub. Although I'm pleased to identify as a feminist—a privilege of education and culture that the majority of women where I come from have not had—I don't feel satisfied with my context for the term.

Working-class women may not be advocating for a cause with words, time, or resources they lack, but they have unrivaled knowledge of how gender affects society. Consider the idea of intersectionality as an example. Although a working-class woman of color may not be familiar with that term, she is the best person to understand how racial, gender, and financial challenges are intertwined.

So there are two types of knowledge: intellectual knowledge, which is the subject of research papers and opinion pieces, and experiential knowledge. Both are crucial, and women from many walks of life may have both. But since knowing is the only form of feminism that many working women have, we hardly ever glorify it.

LEAVING HOME

Parton's career began to take off at the same time as the women's liberation movement, offering an insightful contrast between feminism as a political theory and feminism as it is really practiced today. Parton had little knowledge of the former but was a master at the latter, like most poor women.

Without believing you are on par with males, you will not advance very far as a poor woman. That conviction makes it unlikely that the solution will be a "leaning in," Sandberg's probably wise counsel to middle- and upper-class women hoping to take advantage of the advantages enjoyed by the men in their workplaces and homes. The preferable option for a poor woman is frequently to turn back and leave a hopelessly patriarchal setting that she is unable to resolve with her meager cultural capital.

It was 1964, the year of the presidential election, and the nation was riven by political unrest and tragedy when Parton left Sevier County, Tennessee. Less than a year earlier, President John F. Kennedy had been slain, and young soldiers were returning from Vietnam in caskets.

Parton recalls hearing about Kennedy's passing on her boyfriend's vehicle radio as she was en route to appear on the Cas Walker radio show during a school holiday in her 1994 autobiography, Dolly: My Life and Other Unfinished Business.

In her essay, she stated, "I had loved John Kennedy... in the way one idealist sees another and loves him for that point within themselves that they share. "I didn't know a lot about politics, but I knew that Kennedy wanted to change a lot of things that were unfair and wrong," the author said. However, in response to the news, her boyfriend referred to Kennedy as a "nigger-lovin' son of a bitch." She dumped him right away.
She remembered thinking, "I couldn't believe that young kid with whom I had experienced intimacy and laughter could be so stupid, prejudiced, and inconsiderate.

The 1960s and 1970s women's freedom movement had not yet reached its zenith. The National Organization for Women had not yet formed, but Kennedy had established a panel to examine the position of women. Women from all socioeconomic classes are still forced to live as the wives, mothers, and second-class citizens of rigid, conformist gender norms.

Some of the founding writings of that movement hadn't yet been published when Parton got off the bus in Nashville, but they probably wouldn't have reached Parton anyhow. The women of her lot were too preoccupied with feeding hungry mouths and some were even more cut off from society in a pre-internet rural area to read such literature, which was written in an English dialect they didn't understand. Parton's father, a farmer and occasionally a coal miner who was illiterate due to a lack of education, did not have the privilege of learning to read.

However, Parton was a feminist without having read about it. She indicated that she wanted a better life and believed she deserved it by leaving home alone as a woman with professional goals and no money, even though there was no example of the trip ahead outside her own imagination.

In the meanwhile, there was no more treacherous terrain for a woman to navigate than the city where she would seek that life—the center of country music recording. Nashville was located directly under the thickest glass, despite the fact that America had by that point made a few minor gaps in the ceiling that kept women down.

Patsy Cline, who perished in a plane crash the year before Dolly Parton arrived in town, had lately contested the old-boy network of the industry, where women hardly ever had the lead roles in productions. She ventured to wear pants onstage at the Grand Ole Opry in 1960, and a male emcee drew her aside to scold her in front of the audience. Although Cline, a trailblazer for her gender, was born to take and dish that kind of heat, she was unable to overcome economic inequality. The woman's original record agreement, in the 1950s, granted women half the industry-standard pay rate males received and reserved all publishing rights for her label, according to the PBS documentary American Masters: Patsy Cline. This made her voice subject to the needs of the studio. However, Cline thought it was better than her last employment cutting chicken throats on an assembly line since she was eager to leave her own low, working-class roots in Virginia.

For a female singer-songwriter, it was a tough road, and Dolly Parton's ambitions didn't come true as swiftly as she'd planned. She quickly became so impoverished that she had to steal food from supermarkets or wander through hotel hallways looking for room service trays left outside of doors for pickup.

She gained some local notoriety over the course of a few years by performing mercenary jobs, such as live appearances on early-morning radio shows and a jukebox conference in Chicago. She gained notoriety as the uncredited background singer on the popular pop song "Put It Off Until Tomorrow," which she and her uncle co-wrote and which was nominated BMI Song of the Year. Parton ultimately had the opportunity to record "Dumb Blonde," her debut country song, the following year, in 1967. It reached the Top 10.

The song "Dumb Blonde," which chastises a guy for calling a woman stupid, is the biggest irony in Parton's career. Throughout her career, the motif of a woman outsmarting a guy who undervalues her would resurface. As with most of her future songs, Parton didn't create that song, but she experienced it so fully that she was unable to sing it on television without a man carrying out the exact action the song describes.

The hit song's twenty-one-year-old performer, Dolly Parton, donned a tight orange dress with a high neckline to the syndicated The Bobby Lord Show performance. Although her enormous blond beehive was a few inches higher than the average, there was no sign of the country or the garish appearance for which she is now famous.

But when Parton talked, her East Tennessee accent and the fact that she was more competent than the male host both came through. Someone had prepared a silly introduction to her performance where Lord was allegedly going to deftly refer to her as a dumb blonde with a well-timed pause, as in, "Why don't you go sing, dumb blonde," as opposed to, "Why don't you go sing "Dumb Blonde." Parton played her part by being perplexed and grinning, but even on the second attempt, Lord struggled to deliver the phrase correctly, and the joke failed.

Even yet, taking a chance on those kinds of humiliations in exchange for publicity or a meager payment paid off. Parton noted in her memoirs that Porter Wagoner, whose country music hour was the top-rated nationally syndicated show on television, had been following her work and had noticed "something magical" in her. Will she appear on his show? The wage proposal was for $60,000.

Given the affluence of Wagoner and the show, it was a rip-off, but in Parton's eyes, it was a fortune. Yes, of course, she replied.

Parton's major gamble—leaving home as a young adult without even two dimes to rub together at a time when her own mother in a Smoky Mountain holler was already married and had two kids—had paid off. However, she had found herself in a different kind of bind: a long, frequently unpleasant stint working alongside the male host's loud ego on The Porter Wagoner Show. However, Parton would never again wander the halls of hotels looking for leftovers from room service.

According to an interview Parton gave to Billboard in 2014, she used that first sum of cash to purchase her first brand-new vehicle. By that time, she was married to a man who owned a company that poured concrete, therefore the car was chosen based on his tastes.

Carl exclusively drove Chevrolets at the time, so I presume it was a Chevrolet, Parton claimed.

She didn't know how to drive, much like many other ladies of that era, especially poor ones. She crashed the blue station wagon against the wall of Nashville's Studio A while on her way to record for the first time with Wagoner. There is some lyrical meaning to the fact that she rolled up and broke bricks off a powerful recording studio when she was tearing down walls in the realm of men. The bricks were changed, but they were never quite the same.

She said to Billboard that "when [the studio] used to do tours, they'd go around and say, 'This is where Dolly Parton ran into the wall.'"

HAVING ENOUGH

The majority of poor women's risks don't result in success and wealth. But the lives of the women I grew up with—workers at airplane factories, cafeteria cooks, cashiers at bargain stores, servers at diners, and fast-food employees—all share a common thread of drastic, self-preserving departures. They kept repeating the same phrase throughout the stories they told me about their pasts and present: "I had enough of his shit."

The "he" in the story could be an unfaithful partner, an abusive husband, or a cruel boss. Sometimes a hostile environment was created by a place rather than a person, such as the small Colorado town that shunned my grandmother when she was in her 20s for wearing miniskirts and acting inappropriately in the 1960s, or the Kansas neighborhood where her teenage sister was humiliated for becoming pregnant outside of marriage. They did it because it was required to survive—either physically or psychologically—rather than because it was a positive gesture. Because of my family's predicament, the following man or location was frequently no better than the previous one. They might, however, leave once again, and they did. My grandmother Betty divorced six men by the time she was thirty-two.

She was shot by the first. Her son was taken hostage by the second. Her jaw was broken by the third. The fourth one was a quick business deal: He, a Mexican immigrant, could obtain a US visa if she could prove to the courts that she had a spouse, as an attorney had requested during her attempts to get her son back. The fifth was revealed to have suffered permanent emotional damage while serving in Vietnam. The sixth one verbally attacked Betty and my mother, who was an adolescent at the time.

It wasn't going to get it, as my grandma would remark about any miserable circumstance she left behind.

The majority of that relationship drifting took place before the second-wave feminism's apogee, which Betty was unaware of. She was unaware of the patriarchal background of the marriage institution, which middle-class women in the following decades would learn about in women's studies classes and discuss in gatherings. She had never heard of the term "patriarchy"; I had not either until I was a young lady in college. She was only certain that neither she nor her kids would be treated unfairly by a guy, a town, or a boss.

Jobs and locales turned out to be just as transitory during that time as relationships. With my mother, great-grandmother, and aunts, Betty worked countless jobs and traveled the nation in pursuit of a better location, smoking cigarettes out of a rattled jalopy and wearing a ringless hand.

With that kind of a resume, one may be tempted to assume that a woman can't stay in one place and that, rather than her circumstances, she is always looking for trouble and moving on. She may have been drawn to terrible situations because she lacked regard for herself. But to do so would be to underestimate how many consecutive bad hands a young lady living in poverty in the 1960s might receive.

Betty kept her cards when she eventually received a few decent hands. She became a state employee at the age of thirty and remained one for decades until her retirement. A job-training grant for women helped her secure a position as a secretary in the Kansas courts system in downtown Wichita. She soon after met my grandfather, a funny, loving farmer who was the first guy to treat her well in her life. They were married and spent the next 22 years living on his farm together till he passed away.

A middle-class woman might organize political meetings and write letters to local newspaper editors demanding her daughter's basketball team receive coverage on par with her son's; she might fight for equality with men in her corporate office and demand that her husband change diapers and vacuum; she might donate money to Planned Parenthood and use some of her hard-earned savings to spend a weekend marching with other women in the nation's capital. All of these noble deeds entail using an institution's already-existing agency to effect change. This middle-class woman is fighting to advance women's status in the workplace, the home, politics, and public policy. She might stay and change those realms since they have become welcoming enough to her.

For the poor woman, there is significantly less social, economic, or cultural capital available for internally reversing a situation. She might, however, have a car and just enough cash for gas to get out of a predicament.

No matter one's financial situation, there is a strong sense in leaving the s**t for someone else to fix. When I taught at a tiny university with an odd history of tenured female professors quitting, I was aware of this. Even middle-class women, those of us who could strive to change the societies in which we live, occasionally come to the realization that we would dedicate our entire lives to make even the slightest change. Are our lives worth the inch? Five months after being given tenure, I quit.

Several of my female middle-class pals were concerned that I had become insane. I had no other sources of income or prospects at the moment. I did have a lot of school loan debt and a mortgage. But I soon discovered that the misogyny I experienced on the job at that university was on par with the ass-beatings I had endured for seven years as a server. In the end, it was not going to succeed. My mother and Grandma Betty were two women who never asked questions and merely nodded softly in agreement with a profound knowing.

At that point, I abandoned the larger institution of colleges and universities that I had used to escape poverty. After a few years back in the doldrums, it turned out to be a wise choice—possibly the most audacious feminist act I will ever commit, and one through which dreams were realized. I owe the poor women in my family for giving me the courage I needed. A woman who is confident in her worth should occasionally lean in. She should, however, occasionally simply quit.

As the young female co-star of Porter Wagoner on a program that retained his name, Parton would come to understand the conflict between those two approaches.

Wagoner, a successful businessman who enjoyed a string of country singles in the 1950s, took advantage of the new television medium before most musicians did. He was a self-made man with an ego that outshone his Nudie Cohn suits, which were embellished with rhinestones. He was born in a little town in the southern Missouri

Ozarks. Being tall, with a long face, a yellow pompadour, and a solemn temperament, he had a commanding physical presence. Dolly, on the other hand, was five feet tall, dressed modestly, and smiled brightly and sincerely. Later in her career, Parton would become recognized for her dazzling appearances, but on Wagoner's show, it was obvious that he valued his image more than she did.

Wagoner was old enough to be her father, but Parton had been chosen to play the role of a romantic lead in a variety show. She was supposed to accompany him when singing duets in which a man and woman act as lovers. Wagoner, though, would receive more than he anticipated.

Audiences were initially dubious about Parton succeeding Norma Jean as the female co-star, but they soon began to care more about Parton than they did about the host. She and Wagoner both released solo albums in addition to the duets, butchers sold better. Both of them wrote songs, butchers were superior.
According to Parton's memoirs, Wagoner tried to firmly control Parton and her career the more threatened he felt. He told her what she should sing, what she should write, if she was allowed to compose, and who would publish the songs. Parton described being frightened of conflict in her memoirs. Wagoner was a blustery screamer who needed to be pumped up, but she was a steady, compassionate friend who was willing to offer a lot. Wagoner was a troubled soul who needed to be blown up. Their relationship had all the ingredients for typical abuse.

Wagoner used every trick in the book of the domineering man to keep other business-related male influences out of her life. Billy Owens, who had long served as her musical mentor and an industry supporter, was shunned by him. He requested she switch from Monument Records, where Wagoner worked as an intermediary in the contract, to RCA, and leave her close friend and producer Fred Foster behind. Yes, he wanted her to succeed because it would assist him. But as her popularity shone, he grew more and more aggressive and possessive.

He draped his long arm across her petite shoulders in a jealous-boyfriend move that many women would know during a 1971 television interview they made together that is now available online. He also instructed her when to talk.

Parton asserts that they were not romantically involved and has never referred to his behavior as sexual harassment. However, there will always be romance rumors involving male and female co-stars. Parton made a suggestion in her memoirs that Wagoner might have fostered those rumors. Tammy Wynette occasionally stood in for Parton on the program, and Parton recalled Wynette's worry that Wagoner may use his tales of sexual conquest to harm both of their reputations.

Tammy once asked me, "What if Porter claims we all slept with him?" while we were conversing. Parton composed. "I told Tammy, "Don't worry. "'Half the people will think he's lying and the other half will just think we have bad taste,'" said the speaker.

Wagoner's power maneuvers may have made Parton grin, but a closer look at their on-screen conversation reveals a woman who is aware of what is happening and will respond to any slight with a subtle move capable of shattering Wagoner's flimsy façade of poise.

Parton continues, "I need a security blanket," drawing what appears to be a line for her own self-preservation. They next sing "Her and the Car and the Mobile Home," a song from their 1972 duet album The Right Combination—Burning the Midnight Oil, as Wagoner hammers away on the strings. The song tells the story of an unfaithful husband who discovers his suffering wife has abandoned him when he returns home.

In the same program, Wagoner introduces Parton's solo performance and cracks a joke she finds offensive. She responds off-camera, jokingly disputing what he stated. His broad smile temporarily fades.

He flatly commands, "Shut up," after which Parton performs her timeless hit, "Tennessee Mountain Home," with her trademark wide smile.

Perhaps it's no surprise that in that episode from 1972, the year Parton's five-year contract with Wagoner expired, Wagoner's hostility is on full display.

Wagoner persuaded Parton to continue working after the expiration of her contract, but their conflict only grew. In one especially difficult interaction from a 1973 episode, the nice girl Wagoner hired is now a feisty woman who is just about done, which Rolling Stone explored in 2016.

Wagoner puts his arm around Parton's shoulders and declares, "We're back again." "This is me and my sidekick. She simply gave me a sidekick. Parton pretends to strike Wagoner as he flinches and gasps, and the two of them laugh and smile.

As he turns to face him, Parton looks up. "Not yet, but I think I will after that," she replies.

Wagoner moves his arm away from her, and this time his smile fades from his face more noticeably.

He stutters, "Ohhh." "Dolly Parton, you'll be in trouble if you ever hit me and I find out."

The conversational duet "Run That by Me One More Time," in which a man lies about his whereabouts and a woman lies about her spending, has them smiling and swaying within a matter of seconds.

Wagoner invites a spectator to join them onstage at the conclusion of the song. Jimmy Dean, a famous country singer, appears in the scene as a huge man in a hulking blue suit walking toward Dolly Parton while holding out his arms. She giggles and pushes against him to keep their torsos apart for an uncomfortable amount of time while he forces himself onto Parton. After sparring verbally with Wagoner, Parton was physically confronted by a man whose name was synonymous with sausage.

Parton may not be able to inspire the same kind of bravery and audacity in us now. Despite having left a world of physical labor, she faced few safeguards when she entered environments where men predominated. She would consider it a benefit that she got married soon after coming in Nashville because, while many men would treat her poorly if she were single, others would refrain from bothering her if she were wearing a wedding band, either because they perceive her as being "claimed" or out of concern that her husband might give her a whoopin'.

However, Wagoner was seen as Parton's spouse in the media, and the same brashness that drove him crazy also enabled him to make a sizable profit. In the final line of "Run That by Me One More Time," Wagoner states in his speaking voice in the recording studio, "I ought to box your jaws." "Aw," says Parton in reply, "you'd hit your mama before you hit me."

A distinguishing feature of female country music and the working-class women's culture is this comic boldness in the face of an unfunny menace. You may remember that my granny Betty actually had her jaw broken by her husband while she was leaving him. He was going to be her third ex-husband when she was twenty-three, destitute, and the mother of two children. She laughed as she told me about it.

I put my palm on her chin as she murmured, "Feel this," and she jutted her chin in my direction. When she moved her lower jaw to one side, it made a loud click and was slightly misaligned, as it had been for almost fifty years. That was a gift from a sweetheart of mine.

Betty had lived a life that, like the lives of so many other women, some people in more privileged classes describe as "like a country song"—a reductive assessment. The tales of the women they knew who were normally unheard in society were purposefully recounted by artists like Dolly Parton. To put it another way, the song came after the living. Whether it be through the songs she wrote or the person she is, Parton has never wavered from representing them. She would reveal herself to be the woman from "Her and the Car and the

Mobile Home," who steals the trailer in the end, on Wagoner's program.

ESCAPE ARTISTS

Most musical genres contain lyrics about people packing up and leaving, but the leaving that occurs in country music has a uniquely impoverished, female, and American feel to it. You may imagine the woman in these songs as the female version of the wandering outlaw who sings about honky-tonks, railways, and gambling.

Those men's songs frequently suggest that a woman is patiently waiting at home, admirably enduring her partner's neglect. The rough-hewn ladies I know resemble those from the early 1990s more. In the hit song "Watch Me" by Lorrie Morgan (also, ironically, written by males), she promises to leave her boyfriend despite his skepticism, and you can tell by the tone of her voice who of them is right. Trisha Yearwood drives a 1969 Tempest down Highway 40 toward Nashville in the song "Wrong Side of Memphis" because she has nothing to lose and wants to fulfill her childhood ambition of appearing on the Grand Ole Opry. The personal liberties and vastness of the United States, which are more frequently linked with male experiences, enable such departures.

Additionally, leaving permeates the larger roots music community. Tracy Chapman, in her two biggest singles, asks skeptically for "one good reason to stay" and declares her intention to escape a difficult situation with a fast automobile and some cash she saved working at the convenience store.

The middle-class woman, whose existence is more solid and anchored and includes a good job, a gym membership, and a leadership position in community organizations, is more place-bound than the hard-up woman. The impoverished woman will have a tougher problem gathering the funds necessary to travel, but in spirit she is what they refer to as a flight risk, and there is more than just a wayward guy that she longs to fly away from. Small town, harsh work, and an entire class describe it.

In their song "Boston Town," the bluegrass group Della Mae portrays a member of the famous Bread and Roses Strike of 1912 in Lawrence, Massachusetts, where nearly 30,000 textile workers representing a wide range of ethnicities, the majority of whom were female immigrants, banded together to protest hazardous working conditions and demand higher pay.

"Boston Town" is a unique celebration of the fortitude of working-class women who are at the heart of social change—exactly the subject of many of Parton's early songs. She simply informs them directly, in the homes and hearts of women.

Early songs by Parton likewise portray the oppressed lady in the pre-progress state. Instead of stories about vehicles and horizons, these are gloomy, understated acknowledgments of situations that a woman could need to flee. Young Parton frequently sings about women who are confined to a state of social and economic oppression.

"Just Because I'm a Woman," Parton's first success with RCA, was released in 1968.

revealed the sexual double standards that ethically disqualified the women who shared a bed with playboy guys yet encouraged them to be playboys. The song had a conventional country guitar strum, yet the ideals that Dolly Parton promoted in Nashville through the lyrics were just as radical as the feminist literature produced by radical small presses and academic institutions.

Parton continues singing about a woman who had her reputation destroyed and had her sexual partner go so that she could propose marriage to a virgin "angel."

According to Parton, the song's inspiration came from her own experiences. In her memoirs, she said that she had grown up testing the bounds of propriety in the devout backwoods of Tennessee, where using a charred matchstick as eyeliner was the stuff of scandal.

Soon after arriving in Nashville, she met a lovely man named Carl Dean at a washing facility, and he quickly realized they were meant to be married. A woman as nice as Dolly, he reasoned, must also be a "nice girl." He made the decision to inquire about her previous relationships eight months after their wedding.

She was really happy when, a few years after its release in the US, the song she wrote as a result of that marital argument, "Just Because I'm a Woman," made it to the Top 20 chart in South Africa. In the Rolling Stone profile, she yelled about it, "All those oppressed women!"

With the title tune of her 1975 album "The Bargain Store," which Wagoner and Bob Ferguson co-produced at RCA, Parton continued to refute the false saint-or-whore dichotomy. A woman compares herself to goods that have been used and even destroyed but are still in acceptable shape in the song, a haunting yet confident plea to her potential lover. The audacious chorus even suggests something other than an open heart when it says, "The bargain store is open—come inside."

According to Parton in her interview with Entertainment Weekly, "a lot of stations wouldn't play it because they thought it was about a whore." Nevertheless, the song climbed the charts to become her fifth number-one single.

The Fairest of Them All, a 1970 album by Dolly Parton that was recorded approximately halfway through her tenure on The Porter Wagoner Show, is composed entirely of her original songs and documents the horrors that women who are economically and physically dependent on males must undergo. Of course, the album's name alludes to a sexist fairy tale; on the cover, Dolly Parton smiles into a mirror with the innocent Snow White in mind, but her long ruff conjures the evil queen.

In the movie "Daddy Come and Get Me," a grown daughter asks her father to save her from a mental hospital where her husband has put her so that he can have a relationship with someone else. That song highlighted the long-standing psychiatric practice of labeling a sane woman "crazy" and institutionalizing her when it suited a man's agenda. This practice was still prevalent in the 1970s.

The third song on Fairest features a woman warning her lover that she will break up with him if he tries to control or modify her. When the pull of ownership becomes overwhelming, Parton promises to move on.

In "I'm Doing This for Your Sake," a lady breaks her heart when she tells a baby that she must give it up for adoption because the father fled; in order to get her in bed, he told her that they'd get married and then separate once he learned she was pregnant.

"Down from Dover," the album's standout tune, has the pop-country feel of the '70s with steel guitar, tambourine, backup vocals, and a hint of harpsichord laid over a mid-tempo melody. But at that early stage of her career, when the ghosts of the ladies whose destinies she has escaped are still chasing her, it is typical Parton storytelling. A teenage girl becomes pregnant in the narrative, and her parents disgrace her and force her to leave the family. The father of the child has left town, giving her the impression that he will return to propose to her before she begins to show. She cries out for the boy to come back, but the seasons pass silently. In the fall, she gives birth to a stillborn daughter without medical assistance after going into labor alone: "I guess in some strange way she knew she'd never have a father's arms to hold her / And dying was her way of telling me he wasn't coming down from Dover."

Parton has stated that the song, which was recorded by Marianne Faithfull and Nancy Sinatra, is still one of her favorites. A few years prior to releasing it, she had been bobbing her head to the male-written song "Dumb Blonde," which had some snark but lacked the gravitas Parton brought with her from Sevier County's hollers. She was now relating gothic tales of ladies that were too real to be broadcast on the radio. Parton recalled that "Dover"'s contentious issue of unmarried pregnancy prevented RCA from releasing it as a single.

When presenting the song, she has informed crowds that she had composed it when she was just eighteen years old, but that it would take her until she was thirty before society would accept hearing her sing it.

Parton left her home in the 1960s and 1970s to pursue fame in Nashville. But in other ways, she was in the same predicament as a prostituted child living in a shanty in Sevier County. At the time, there were very few female country music stars; all were manufactured and managed by males in suits. She took up golf since it was such a man's world and she wanted to stay in the know.

She once made a birdie on a par three hole, and her book claims that she was so pleased with herself that she had the Titleist ball mounted. Wagoner promised to accomplish it and then presented her with a plaque without the unique golf ball—instead, it was an Arnold Palmer ball. One of several passive-aggressive jabs, according to Parton, was involved in the event.

Back in the woods, Parton hadn't become entangled by a thoughtless boy and a teenage pregnancy. Instead, she was forced to work for and be contractually obligated to a guy who thought of himself as her spouse, her father, and her boss. That man just so happened to be her male counterpart in certain ways: a guitar-playing, talent-filled, tenacious country kid who worked hard and achieved success. What she had entered was the more affluent, show industry equivalent of the life she had intended to leave behind. The sorrows of women who weren't as fortunate are reflected in her songs from that era rather than the victory of an independent woman who "got out"—a potent expression of solidarity with her unfortunate sisters back home, but also perhaps a disguised revelation about her relationship with Porter Wagoner.

Parton's bus may have been driven by women's protests, marches, and sit-ins while she traveled the nation performing those songs. Parton had little experience with the world of direct political activism, self-awareness of one's own power in a democracy, and the use of data and testimonials to influence public opinion. She was aware of what my grandmother Betty had taught me about female life: that it is a private, intimate experience in which you will eventually be shaken to your core by an inner vibration that, if you don't leave, would cause you to crumble.

The knowledge that women who move around can't be controlled is something society will work to suppress. If the institutions remain, everyone wins: They perform both the emotional and physical labor in the heterosexual marriage. The low-paying occupations where they complete their work and are also required to set up the birthday cupcakes in the conference room. Parenting, where parents continue to change the majority of diapers regardless of who "brings home the bacon"—and they continue to fry the majority of bacon, as well.

When Parton left Tennessee in 1964, her small community definitely begged her to "stay," even if it was just by pressuring her to settle down and have children and by making fun of her lofty aspirations to become a celebrity. Porter Wagoner instructed her in simple legal language to "stay" ten years later. That still serves as the message for all women, in many ways. However, because to the exits made by women before us, we can now enjoy songs that are about leaving. These songs convey tales that feel plausible.

The leaving of a woman is a statement. Many of them—particularly by the underprivileged women, Black women, Brown women, queer women, and transgender women—have gone unnoticed as more powerful individuals preach about equality at podiums next to government buildings.

Dolly Parton was speaking into a different type of microphone as Betty, a woman around her age, was watching. When I was a child, I discovered Grandma Betty's old records scrawled in pen with last names I had no idea she had ever possessed. When I was a little child, I had thoughts of moving away, and no one in my family or the rural towns ever laughed or tried to tell me that I couldn't. Where I lived, "feminism" was never discussed. However, the poor females who came before me had already made a rut on the road.

AN OPEN DOOR

Parton's time with Wagoner makes me think of the opening stanza of a well-known poem by Adrienne Rich from 1978, "A wild patience has taken me this far." The middle-aged speaker of that poem, written by one of the nation's foremost public intellectuals and second-wave feminists, realizes that her greatest strength lies in her ability to hold simultaneously opposing emotions such as anger and tenderness, sadness for the past and hope for the future, and pride and pain from working alone for a lifetime.

Due to her commercial connection with Wagoner, Parton had improved her financial stability. Of course, her pay was scandalously inadequate. But like many working women today, she felt simultaneously appreciative of and surprised to be paid at all.

Parton furnished and decorated her parents' home for the first Christmas after landing the role on Wagoner's show. She made sure the girls had plenty of the pink and frilly items Parton had yearned for as a young girl while her younger siblings were still living at home. This idea of "girl stuff" can be offensive to feminists. The problem for Parton was not that these things were imposed upon her, but rather that she was denied access to them. Pink ruffles weren't merely a gender trap in a country where women worked side by side with men and had no money for gowns or makeup, even if they wanted them.

Grandma Betty never became wealthy or even what most people would consider "comfortable," but over time, her work in Kansas' criminal justice system gave her enough money to be able to pay her bills while a meager pension built. She used to wear an emerald ring all the time when I was a child, so one day I asked her who had given it to her.

She admitted to me, "I've had it since I started working in the courts." "I paid for the damn thing myself because I've always wanted an emerald ring." She didn't have to explain to me the significance—that each other ring she had placed on a finger had been given to her by a man—to me.

Parton gained more than just financial stability from her appearance on Wagoner's show. She amassed accolades with both of their names on them; in 1968, they were recognized as the best vocal group of the year by the Country Music Association. And when he wanted to, Wagoner could really fight for her. Their relationship grew stressful, but it also had its positive points.

Wagoner organized "Dolly Parton Day" in 1970 in her hometown, enlisting famous Nashville musicians to perform in Sevierville. A Real Live Dolly, an outstanding live CD, included the performance in its recording. Wagoner made money off of that apparent unselfish ode to Parton and her heritage, of course, but according to her perspective, he also had a true love and respect for her. It was shared.

She described him as "a Missouri boy with a dream" in her memoirs. Few others could comprehend each one of them because of their unique life paths, but they understood one another.

Wagoner might be a terrific educator as well. She had been working professionally since she was a young child for almost twenty years by the time they became partners. She still had a lot to learn, though, about entertaining a large audience.

When someone disrupts a quiet moment with a shout and Dolly Parton responds with a line, you can still feel his influence on a Parton performance today. He taught her how to handle a commotion in the audience.

Parton has long been known to don a Nudie outfit, so Wagoner may have also given her taste in rhinestones and over-the-top hair.
Wagoner left her with a number of impressions, but perhaps his admirers were the most significant.

Parton was unfamiliar with that name. She recalled it when, according to her, she sat down to write a song a year later and was motivated by a flirty relationship between her husband and an auburn-haired employee of their bank. The persona of the woman who posed a threat required a name. She chose the name after talking to a teenage fan she met while touring with Wagoner, and it ended up having such a catchy sound that it inspired countless musicians from different genres to cover the song for decades.

The song "Jolene" from 1973 was a crossover pop hit that peaked at number one on the country charts and received a Grammy nomination. Although it wasn't her first solo victory, something about the occasion felt unique.

Parton gained confidence. She had been patient with Wagoner throughout the years, but she never lost her own wild side. The two had been circling behind the scenes despite their broad smiles on camera and on stage.

They ultimately had opposing goals: she wasn't interested in being kept, while he wanted to keep her.

She had been working on the show for seven years by that point, which was two more than her five-year contractual commitment. It appears that she stayed because she felt obligated to a man who said she owed him her career. Parton is not the kind to express her connection with Wagoner as anything other than a godsend that occasionally seemed like a pain in the ass. But just as the songs she wrote during those times, her comments about them have a grim undertone.

So, ten years after leaving rural East Tennessee, in her late 20s, she found the courage to quit something that no longer served her needs. As the renowned duet, they were traveling and performing live, Parton said in her book. In front of the hotel, a cab was waiting with the door opened for her.

She was worried that RCA would lose interest in her. Wagoner had subtly implied that without him, the label wouldn't be interested in her. She met with businessmen Ken Glancy and Mel Ilberman and requested a conference in New York.

It's difficult to understand how uncertain a woman who would create a commercial empire may feel. But it is understandable that she would not be aware that the world regarded her as highly as she did.

No matter how resilient you are, years of criticism from a manipulator of emotions like Wagoner will have a negative impact on your mind.

Parton revealed to Wagoner that she had written the heartbreaking farewell song "I Will Always Love You" for him to mark her exit from the program.

A song that potent is not created without having truth in every line. But think what that kind of farewell meant. No fool, Parton has long since created a music publishing firm and held the rights to any recordings of her songs. She therefore owed her sad farewell, and Wagoner had no right to it. Every cent that was made went directly into her account, not his.

In her first season away from Wagoner, Parton toured as Mac Davis' opening act. I picture her driving down the freeway in a bus with butterflies and the word "Dolly" emblazoned on the side, riding with her new band, Gypsy Fever. The renowned steel guitarist Don Warden, who was from Wagoner's hometown and had played in his performance and original trio, may have been riding along. He had grown close to Parton, and when she left Wagoner, he followed suit, taking on the role of her manager for close to fifty years.

As the bus sped through a field she wasn't working in and a cafe where she would never have to wait tables, Parton must have experienced a new lightness. She was twenty-eight years old and, for the first time in her life, unbound by a place, a guy, or a contract. When the DJ reveals that "I Will Always Love You" has reached the top of the charts, I picture "I Will Always Love You" playing on the bus radio and the Gypsy Fever musicians cheering. I envision Parton singing along to the 1972 Carly Simon smash song "You're So Vain" while it plays, laughing hysterically at one specific lyric in the chorus: "I'll bet you think this song is about you, don't you?"

Parton recounted how thrilled she was when Elvis Presley requested to record "I Will Always Love You" in a 2006 interview with CMT. Presley was already a legend, but she was already a star. Finally,

"Colonel" Tom Parker, Presley's manager, tried to pull a shady move on her just before the recording session.

When Parton re-recorded "I Will Always Love You" in 1982, it once again reached the top of the charts, making it the only country song in history to do so in two different decades. The song achieved this feat a third time in 1992 when Whitney Houston turned it into a mainstream smash for the soundtrack to The Bodyguard. As a result, Parson's farewell present to the guy who would have kept her in his bed became one of the most popular songs in music history. She continues to cash the checks.

Parton was able to leave Wagoner, reject Elvis, and go on to become not just a successful performer but also a business titan because she had the courage to follow her intuition and upset a strong man in the process.

She vanished, and Wagoner retaliated by filing a vehement lawsuit. He insisted that because he had contributed so significantly to her growth, he was entitled to a share of all the money she would earn going forward as an entertainment. Although Parton had good reason to be concerned as a woman facing the possibility of a courtroom with a male judge, that argument could seem to be lost today. Parton offered to settle for a rumored $1 million rather than take Wagoner to court. Wagoner accepted the offer.

Over the years, Parton and Wagoner would make up and get back together numerous times, even making fun of their past relationship. Parton said to the audience during a 1995 Wagoner roast, "I knew he had balls when he sued me for a million dollars when he was only paying me thirty dollars a week."

Over the years, Parton would continue to remember Wagoner with a combination of blunt remarks and sincere appreciation.

PUNCHING OUT

Feminist activism was transforming the globe as Parton left Wagoner. In 1973, the Supreme Court issued its decision in Roe v.

Wade, potentially saving the lives of many of the young, expectant, and abandoned protagonists of Parton's early songs. The Women's Educational Equity Act also provided funding for the creation of less discriminatory instructional materials the following year, making forced unpaid maternity leave unlawful.

The United States did not suddenly become a bright, simple place for women, even though many of those benefits have been long-lasting. In particular, reproductive rights have long been the focus of political tactics known as "death by a thousand cuts."

Similar to how Parton was freed from Wagoner's shackles, she did not experience a conventional, happy ending. A woman can escape the impoverished countryside and a tyrannical male boss, but she cannot leave a sexist and misogynistic culture. successfully reject it consciously every day? Perhaps. exist without it? No.

Parton's lyrics would continue to infuriate powerful men well past the point at which equality had purportedly been attained, not to mention the struggles she undoubtedly fought behind closed doors. The same as "Down from Dover" and "The Bargain Store" did 25 years earlier, she struggled to get her 1991 ballad "Eagle When She Flies," a tribute to the simultaneous vulnerability and inner power of women, played on the radio.

Parton noted in the 2003 Rolling Stone interview that "a lot of DJs wouldn't play [it] because they thought it was such a women's lib song."

You can see where Parton comes from by the fact that she didn't give her own work the "women's lib" title. But you know exactly what it was because men decided that her song shouldn't be heard.

When male DJs threw "Eagle When She Flies" out, Parton responded: President George H. W. Bush and First Lady Barbara Bush watched her perform it at the Country Music Association Awards from the front row. She used the occasion to introduce her song by drawing a contrast between what she wished to elevate and the ultimate symbol of patriarchy—the wealthy, white, male ruler of the globe.

"Everyone was expressing their pride at having the president here. So are we. Very grateful. However, I wanted to do a song tonight, and I want to dedicate this to Barbara Bush," Parton added, her neckline far lower than what Porter Wagoner would have approved and her platinum wig nearly as high as some of her old beehives. "We all agree that there are some amazing men in the world, but there are just as many outstanding women. She, those like her, and females from all backgrounds... So, this is for all the women in the world and here tonight.

The stage lit up to reveal a sizable, mostly white choir of newly arriving women dressed cheesily as members of professional trades: the businesswoman with shoulder pads, the delivery driver in a brown jumpsuit holding a box, the soldier in fatigues, the astronaut, policewoman, surgeon, construction worker, and even a director. The teacher, the nurse, the rancher, and the diner server with her tray were among the positions that women had previously held. However, the American president, who received everything while Parton worked for hers, had to take the images into account. He watched from the front row, captive in front of the cameras, while the farmer's uneducated daughter assured him that his wife was on par with him. Despite the absurd images, it was a beautiful presentation that, even when viewed today, still feels revolutionary.

That was over thirty years after Parton, then a youngster with a guitar, left Sevierville, Tennessee. Sexual harassment in the workplace was illegal at the time of the CMA Awards performance, and more women were making country music recordings. Since then, women have advanced even further in many areas. But some of us spend so much time debating feminist policies that we forget to take a hard look at how we live our lives. What kind of country music may be composed about us? Would they focus on the trapped woman or the one who manages to escape?

Whether or not she has her own work, you may know a wealthy lady with a college degree who has a hospitable, philandering husband who pays the bills but treats her like a trophy or a maid. She might feel content enough to carry on in her current situation. While picking up her husband's dry cleaning, she might even wear a T-shirt with the word "feminist" on it. She may be familiar with words that a poor woman cannot describe, and she may write a furious Facebook post about our misogynistic president.

A poor mother, hoping to find some goddamn respect for herself and her children, is currently leaving a door with nothing to her name and beginning her new life. The woman who advocates for feminism may not always be the same woman who demands equality in private.

Leaving was a revolutionary act, whether it was poor Dolly Parton refusing to stay in a holler or wealthy Dolly Parton gazing at Porter Wagoner's studio door. It is a force that, over time, has driven wealthy firms, coal companies, and textile mills to their knees when working women have had enough and poverty and gender interact.

In a Roseanne episode, the titular character confronts a sexist, verbally abusive supervisor who breaks his word and reinstates harsh production quotas for female workers in a plastics plant in a small Illinois town. I can still remember the joy I had watching that episode as a child.

When Parton punched her card and left the Porter Wagoner music factory, she was paving the way for female musicians in a field where they still infrequently played as the headliners.

The words "Dolly & Loretta & Patsy & Tammy" are written in large letters on a stylish T-shirt that is occasionally worn by young women.
Consider it a reminder to leave a generous tip for the next woman who serves you at a diner like the ones on the Great Plains where my grandma used to bus tables or for the cleaning lady who lugs a bucket onto and off of Greyhound buses like Cline used to do in the South when you see it. She owes feminism a debt, and there's a high chance she's putting money aside to advance. You wouldn't want to lean into her life.

Chapter 3:
Becomes the Boss

Three irate women confront their male boss in the 1980 film 9 to 5, who insults, gropes, and berates them. The film provided for many viewers the first expression and denunciation of an openly, dangerously sexist office culture that had long been accepted as "the way things are" or "boys being boys." It served as a parable that imparted lessons to both men and women.

It wasn't difficult for Dolly Parton to portray the objectified secretary of the boss. She had left The Porter Wagoner Show just a few years before after working under one of Nashville's most notorious male egos for years.

Perhaps for this reason, out of the three strong female leads (Parton, Jane Fonda, and Lily Tomlin), the portrayal by the actress who has the least acting experience is, in my opinion, the most convincing.

Of course, Fonda and Tomlin were aware of sexism. And Tomlin, the daughter of a manufacturing worker who momentarily left the South for stable employment in Detroit, like Parton's father did, undoubtedly had intimate knowledge of the linkages between gender and economic difficulties. But there's something particularly sparkling about Parton on screen, and it isn't just her frosty eye makeup.

It's because she was beginning the phase of her career when she would transition from a movie star to a business mogul and a household name. She would perform all of it while wearing a massive platinum-blond wig, skin-tight attire, and plenty of cleavage.

She was probably a third-wave feminist who was born a generation earlier and who concurrently embraced gender performance before it became a political act. I was one of the rural girls watching.

I recently watched the movie 9 to 5 with a group of boisterous women in an Austin, Texas theater. The movie is commonly regarded as a comedy, and that is how I had recalled it from television broadcasts when I was younger. However, when I rewatched it as a woman, I had a rush of nausea brought on by traumatic memories whenever Parton's character was physically grabbed by her boss. When the main characters fantasize about murder and giggle when they load what they believe to be their boss's dead body into a car trunk, women in the crowd cheered. I came to understand that it is among the darkest films ever created regarding the experience of women.

Furthermore, it is still terribly relevant. The US president portrays the repulsive male boss 36 years after the movie's debut. Donald Trump, a reality television star who enjoyed saying "you're fired," once told a contestant that she would look nice on her knees. He reportedly had a propensity of entering the beauty pageants he owned when contestants were getting dressed. 9 to 5 feels so politically charged right now that one wonders if a major studio would still approve it.

I was born in the same year as 9 to 5 came out, so I roughly match Parton's age in the movie at the time. I also happen to be what people still referred to as "a professional woman" during my youth and adolescence in the 1980s and 1990s. I've worked hard to become financially independent since I was 18 years old, am happily divorced without children, and am more motivated by professional ambitions than home ones.

I now see myself and other women of my generation as the cultural children of the 9 to 5 industry. We developed amid a perplexing stew of antiquated social norms and new social freedoms. The new image of the modern woman that society was adopting was one in which she left in the morning to work as a doctor, engineer, or police officer. But did she enjoy baking as well? Of course, it's possible to like cooking, wear heels, and engage in a variety of other stereotypically "feminine" activities without being any less of a feminist. Today's mainstream culture seems to be unambiguous about that. The conflict that defined women in the late 20th century, however, was that they were praised for becoming anything they want while also receiving criticism regardless of how they went about it. Men who felt frightened by them viewed them as strident Amazons if they surged into places of commerce or government; women who felt threatened by them looked completely past them if they were wearing low-cut tops and tight pants while making empowered decisions.

A woman's entire existence may be viewed as a purposeful remedy for centuries of unfair treatment because the concept of gender equality both at home and at work was so novel at the time. A little more than ten years after the publication of 9 to 5, in 1992, Hillary Clinton, the first lady of Arkansas and an attorney with a Yale Law School education, received criticism for explaining to reporters covering her husband's presidential campaign why she worked on public policy rather than draperies as the wife of a governor.

Clinton responded, "I suppose I could have stayed in and made tea and cookies. But I made the decision to pursue my career, which I started before my spouse became well-known. She would later run for president herself, twenty-four years later, and that quote—and the widespread pearl-clutching in response to it—would haunt her ever after.
Not because she dislikes baking, but rather because for generations society has given women aprons while resenting their social and political power, Clinton made nasty remarks about baking cookies. Parton fashioned herself as a "floozy" not because she wanted men's praise, but rather because she lost control over men who would have done it for her if she hadn't sexualized herself.

Women were forced to act as reactions to the rapid social advancements that occurred around the turn of the 20th century. If one wants to overcome a disadvantage, it is a dilemma that is inherent in all disadvantages. The female leads in 9 to 5 aren't always murderous criminals. They are unwilling to murder their boss. But they discover that they might have to.

The first draft of the script, according to the original screenwriter Patricia Resnick, was even macabre. Ahead of the film's 35th anniversary, Resnick spoke with Rolling Stone about her desire to create "a very dark comedy in which the secretaries actually tried to kill the boss." In order to make the three characters more likable, certain plot points were reworked as fantasy sequences.

The fact that the main actresses would all be white was probably not even questioned when it came to casting in general. Even now, it's uncommon for a woman of color to be the movie's leading lady, much less play a character who is threatening a white male boss with a gun.

The movie's gender-related points remain relevant, which is another element that hasn't altered. When the film was staged as a Broadway show in 2009, Resnick recalled interactions with the media's skeptics.

"It was really frustrating," she added, "because a lot of the interviews I did with male journalists, the first thing they said was, 'Well, none of those issues are a problem in contemporary life, so how are women of today going to be able to relate to it?'" I believed that it was evident that you couldn't harass someone sexually. Nobody here is a "secretary." What else has changed, though?

I must state that I concur as a woman who has had numerous positions in the workforce for more than twenty years and has never—not once—worked someplace without experiencing some form of harassment or other ill treatment for my gender. I no longer forgo the numerous advantages and security that come with working within an organizational structure in favor of working as a freelance writer, in large part because of the unrelenting emotional drain of being fired, underpaid, gawked at, and viewed as a threat.

In contrast to Resnick's description of our mothers and grandmothers, many of the men who have displeased us at work have done it in far more subdued ways than the bombastic chauvinism of the 9 to 5— often while claiming to be "feminists." For women, the workplace environment can be even riskier because subtle sexism or misogyny can affect you without you even realizing it and is the most difficult to prove.

Every movement for social change, including feminism, inevitably has a gap between what is declared and what is actually happening: between women's rights legislation and enforcement, between policy advancements and cultural advancements. Women in Generation X, of which I am the youngest member, enjoyed more meaningful freedom than their mothers had. We were the first true recipients of Title IX provisions, which guarantee admission to schools and forbid sexual harassment in the workplace. The Violence Against Women Act was being passed when we started our first relationships. But there were many contradictions and holes in the cultural cues we were exposed to as children.

One of my favorite childhood shows, Moonlighting, had Cybill Shepherd as a whip-smart (and damn funny) investigator in an old episode that just astounded me. She is forced to allow the grinning work colleague played by Bruce Willis, with whom she has recently concluded an on-again, off-again romance, into her home. When she asks him to leave, he refuses, slaps her in the face for disagreeing, and she then accepts him into her arms because of his persistence.

My 20th-century child eyes had witnessed a strong woman fighting back before being turned on by a man who was determined enough to prevail. However, when I opened my eyes as an adult in the twenty-first century, I witnessed a dangerously entitled man chasing a woman and not even respecting or believing her when she said "no."

That was the conflict between a woman's new job in the economy and her traditional one in the bedroom that was highlighted by 9 to 5 at the beginning of the 1980s. It was a challenge for female Baby Boomers, and their Generation X kids saw them struggle to make it home in high heels with little time to moan.

Women still experience these problems today and will do so for a long time. The Equal Rights Amendment hadn't yet been repealed, middle-class women were power-walking to work (as impoverished women had been doing all along), and popular culture indicated a profound communal crisis regarding gender. However, 9 to 5 symbolizes a specific period of conflict in the growth of feminism.

A major change in Parton's career also occurred during that decade of transition: from the Carter to the Reagan administrations, from polyester bell bottoms to stone-washed denim, from women's liberation signs to the false belief that freedom had taken place. She had become a successful solo country music artist when she was a young woman in the 1970s, but 9 to 5 made her a mainstream Hollywood sensation and hastened her path to becoming an icon.

At feminist rallies or in overt political activism, Parton never used her stardom to her advantage. But she did pick a film written by one of the most despised feminists of the time—Jane Fonda—from among what must have been a large number of alternatives. Fonda was still a polarizing figure at the time, with her antiwar "Hanoi Jane" scandal still fresh in the public's memory. And Parton agreed to play a woman who lassos her violent boss and shoves a gun in his face in her debut acting performance.

That Parton wanted to play Doralee, the attractive secretary who was sexually harassed by her disgusting male boss and shunned by her female coworkers who propagated the erroneous notion that she was sleeping with him, is undoubtedly no accident.

As one of the other mistreated female employees, Doralee suffered in particular from being labeled a "slut" due to her seductive appearance and other men's untrue allegations that they were banging her. In high school, Parton herself grew accustomed to that.

FEMINIST SWEET SPOT

Despite the conflicting messages of the time, I consider myself fortunate to have grown up in the feminist golden period, which came after the coordinated marches and policy victories of the 1970s but before the full-fledged conservative backlash of the new millennium. Before right-wing extremists developed an effective political strategy for undermining reproductive rights after Roe v. Wade but before that decision. Before online trolls used technology to track, harass, and embarrass individuals, but after women started working in traditionally male-dominated fields in large numbers.

Earlier than when Fox News put their legs in the picture, but before female journalists started presenting shows on major networks.

Women my age, who were children and teenagers in the 1980s and teenagers and young women in the 1990s, may recall that era more for its music, recordings, and television programming than for its adult politics. But there was frequently a definite political undercurrent in what we learned from those albums and TV shows.

Prior to the hot-pink, baby-talk girl power of the Spice Girls and Britney Spears and the overt, unreserved acceptance of the term "feminism" by Beyoncé and the Dixie Chicks, we went through our most formative years. We had a bunch of sassy bitches in pantsuits who were more intelligent than the men they worked with, including Murphy Brown and Dana Scully. Connie Chung and Diane Sawyer read the evening news while sporting large, angular hairstyles. Clair Huxtable and Angela Bower were wearing shoulder pads when they left the house in the role of stylish but unyielding working mothers. Whitney Houston and Selena sang pop songs while wearing leather jackets and exuding a tough sexual strength. Rappers Queen Latifah and Salt-N-Pepa demand respect while wearing baggy pants and sneakers. In combat boots, Shirley Manson and Sinéad O'Connor are asking everyone to get the fuck off the planet.

In terms of pop-country music, a style that is becoming more and more connected with conservatism, that era featured women singing triumphantly about hard-won freedom while wearing rhinestones and fringed leather clothing.

"Girls' Night Out" from the Judds' chart-topping 1984 debut album Why Not Me, which my mother played on vinyl the most when I was a little child, expresses relief from a demanding work week. The Judds perform the line "I've been cooped up all week / I've been working' my fingers to the bone' ' over steel guitar and saloon piano. They are leaving to go out and dance and party while closing the local bar.

I'm done now. The entire song is just for fun, with no reference to meeting a man.

K. T. Oslin reveals that she has begun entertaining younger lovers in 1987's "Younger Men," another popular song that my mother played repeatedly on the tape deck of her car. When she was younger, she remembers giggling at a fact that stated women achieve their sexual prime at age forty and men at age nineteen. The main issue with being a lady of a certain age is the guys of that age, Oslin sings in "Now I'm Staring Forty Right in the Face."

My mother had just entered her mid-20s when that album, 80's Ladies, was released. I only had seven years. But we both enjoyed talking along with the song's spoken aside as Mom drove down the road holding a Marlboro Light in her fingers and I bobbed my head in the passenger seat. Oslin is driving, reversing the traditional gender roles of catcaller in the car and catcalled on the sidewalk: "Blue shorts, no shirt / WOOOO you're lookin' good, darlin'! / That's right—stay in shape."

When we passed a man jogging in blue shorts, we were singing along to that tune and, my hand to God, we both burst out laughing. This was the result of a delightful flood of empowerment flowing from Oslin's musical pen to a broken road in Kansas. I'm not sure how either of us connected to the specific power imbalance in a middle-aged woman singing such lyrics, but a mother in her twenties and her impressionable daughter seemed to have already grasped it.

By that time, Parton had reached middle age and had written songs about sexual power years before her time. As the 1970s came to a close, she started writing upbeat songs like the pop-country hit "Two Doors Down" from the disco-influenced 1978 album Here You Come Again instead of songs about the shattered, wronged women her earlier career had portrayed.

In the song, the singer woman is sobbing over something—likely a breakup—but she decides to stop. She makes her way down the hallway after overhearing a rager. She is requesting a new guy to return to her home with the next verse. The lyrics by Dolly Parton go, "Here we are feeling everything but sorry / We're having our own party two doors down."

Parton, who established a residence in Los Angeles in 1976, was undoubtedly affected by the counterculture movement's teachings of sexual emancipation. But she has talked of having the same sense of freedom and power as a young woman in a little Tennessee town— self-possession before others agreed with her.

It is up to Parton to decide how much of her sexual experience was or wasn't restricted by her monogamous marriage once she moved to Nashville at the age of eighteen in 1964. (2016) She stated, "I said I was married," to the New York Times. ("I didn't say I was dead.") She did, however, exaggerate and emphasize her beauty in novel ways during the colorful 1980s, which suggests that she was sexually finally coming into her own. Her heels went up, and her neckline dropped down.

In 1982, Parton co-starred with Burt Reynolds as the stereotypical heart-of-gold sex worker in The Best Little Whorehouse in Texas, following her portrayal of the misunderstood Doralee in 9 to 5. It's important to note that she is now the queen in the brothel rather than a worker bee. But she would always perceive the world through the metaphor of the oppressed working girl.

The feminism in Dolly Parton's music and persona may have escaped the notice of the time's cultural commentators, but it was obvious behind the scenes. Best Little Whorehouse was released in the same year that Parton requested to meet Ann Richards, a fiery Texas liberal who was running for state treasurer at the time.

When they first met, Scott Newman, a photographer, was documenting a campaign event for Richards at the renowned Driskill Hotel in downtown Austin. He took a picture of the two women standing together: Parton, a new movie star recognized for her take on the same thing, and Richards, a progressive known for her outspoken feminism and great one-liners.

The two women are depicted in a black-and-white portrait, bursting with laughter and nearly identical save for age and body type differences. They both have blond hair that is curled tightly on top of their heads and ruffles on their tops.

Parton would go on to become a pop culture legend, while Richards would go on to become the last woman and the last Democrat to lead the state of Texas. They would grow to be close friends and were both on the rise. Two people with very different journeys but many things in common.

In the more than three decades after that photograph was shot, Texas, country music, and the entire nation have undergone significant transformation. Texas and the rest of the nation have shifted to the right; it's unlikely Ann Richards would prevail in a Texas election today. While Nashville has embraced a number of male musicians, from "bro country" Luke Bryan to old-school, beard-sporting rebel Chris Stapleton, it has snubbed female political renegades like the Dixie Chicks. Years ago, country radio ceased playing Parton's recent music. The Southern Gothic defenses of underprivileged women she wrote in her twenties are unlikely to be broadcast today.

But that fleeting but significant moment in American history that girls like me—at the time a toddler living in a metal trailer on the Kansas prairie—somehow absorbed is there in that 1982 snapshot, in a Southern state capital. A female politician and a female country singer-turned-Hollywood actress were laughing while exchanging respectful looks in the public sphere of power that reactionary twenty-first-century misogyny had not yet extended its male legs to recapture.

BODY POLITICS

Parton was forced to carry a hyper awareness of her physique and its relationship to the environment because of responses to her physical appearance. Every woman experiences the pain of the male gaze, but Parton's story illustrates how humanity may be turned invisible when that stare is a laser beam the size of Earth.

In 1977, when she appeared on The Tonight program, Johnny Carson, who had a reputation for being somewhat of a gentleman, stuttered and remarked, "I have certain guidelines on this show, but I would give about a year's pay to peek under [her top]."

She was unable to avoid being turned into a sort of visual object by a blind man. Singer Ronnie Milsap, who is blind, asked the audience why she wasn't in her braille Playboy in 1978, the year she became the second woman to ever win Entertainer of the Year honors from the Country Music Association (she is now one of seven overall). (Parton had donned a bunny costume for the cover of the magazine that month but declined to pose in a bikini.)

In her 1994 autobiography, Dolly, Parton outlines the challenges she faced at the time without identifying the gendered nature of any of them. These include sexist body-shaming in Hollywood, male business associates who gave her bad advice, her siblings' resentment of her fame and wealth despite her generosity as a family caregiver, and her siblings' resentment of her fame and fortune.

Parton claimed that the shooting of Best Little Whorehouse was particularly difficult due to the negative energy on the set. Her petite, curvy frame was deemed too overweight for the big screen. It makes you cringe to hear Parton describe how uncomfortable she felt while filming take after take of a sequence in which Reynolds's character scoops her up and carries her across a threshold. She admits that she felt like a failure because of her weight as she reflects on the incident, highlighting her own involvement in the situation.

Her relationship to the already problematic issue of a woman's appetite and physical size was exacerbated by Parton's impoverished childhood, during which deprivation and hunger helped shape her personality.

To prevent his eleven surviving children from starving to death, her father worked construction and farmed for decades. A culture and family that were shaped by the Great Depression and even the European famines their ancestors fled will see shrinking size as potentially cause for concern, despite Parton's assertion that she is not underweight for a petite woman and that her "dramatic weight loss" in the 1980s was, for her, a shift to feeling more healthy rather than less.

Meanwhile, as Carson's and Milsap's jokes show, culture made Dolly Parton the punch line of a joke about enormous tits in order to explain how she could have a quick intellect, a gorgeous face, a creative genius, and a huge rack all rolled into one.

Parton underwent breast augmentation surgery not long after she "lost the weight" during that decade, which she has briefly described in her book and other places. While her breasts might now be referred to as "fake," images from the beginning of her career demonstrate that they are roughly the same size as they were when they were "real." People find the final image shocking—a petite woman with breasts that don't appear to fit her frame. However, it makes sense for a woman whose mere mention led to boob jokes to reclaim not only the joke but the boob as well—perhaps to make it apparent that the joke's punchline didn't make her feel ashamed.
When questioned about the difficult contrast between her origins in poverty, her work as a musician and company owner, and her fame as a female sex symbol, Parton invariably grinned and chuckled. But even a woman who "made it" because of her inherent tenacity is affected by similar influences.

It was a difficult time for the women who paved the way for Parton; a path that was particularly perilous and obstructed for women of color, lesbian women, and anyone who did not fit the cisgender, straight, white pattern preferred by American power structures. The decade was full of conflicting messages for any lady following that path: Work at a "man's job" for less money than men. Wear high heels to click lightly along the corridor while also evoking a man's might by donning shoulder pads. Be self-sufficient enough to drive to work, report to a male employer, and prepare your husband's dinner once you both arrive home from work.

In the past thirty years, that jumble of expectations hasn't altered much, but in the 1980s, it had a freshness that sent American culture into a tailspin and brought even tough-as-nails Parton to her knees. Because she serves as everyone else's safety net in her environment, such a lady frequently pays a heavy price. So who is responsible for her care?

When Parton was in her thirties and in the early 1980s, she went through her darkest time: a mental and emotional breakdown during which she considered committing herself. Her own downfall coincided with the loss of the Equal Rights Amendment in 1982, which was the first significant win for the anti-feminist movement.

The late talent scout Sandy Gallin, who also oversaw Michael Jackson's career, is mentioned in Parton's book as a source of caring advice to assist her get through her serious depression. But in the end, Parton was forced to do what so many women are: burn everything down and start over in order to discover a life that suits them rather than everyone else.

At that time, Parton let go of a few employees, including band members and an accounting firm that kept forgetting that she made all the decisions and paid for them herself. She has stated that she also underwent a partial hysterectomy, however she has not fully explained why. Getting off the then-available high-estrogen birth control pills was one positive outcome she has observed. It served as a moment of closure over her decision to forgo having children.

Parton recovered from the emotional collapse by cleaning the house in her band, her company, her cabinets, her veins, and even her own womb. Her body and brain began to align, and her business started to grow in a crescendo that hasn't stopped since.

From an impoverished rural girl to a Nashville aspirant, from Porter Wagoner's micromanaged co-star to a crossover solo artist, from small-screen singer to big-screen actress, Parton has been actively, purposefully growing since youth. She had hit her emotional bottom, acquired the degree of fame and money she had worked so hard to achieve throughout her life, and was now the same person she had always been—yet psychologically reborn. What would the next objective be? Even though she was in the driver's seat, she had done the best a woman could to rule a man's world, only to discover that it still treated her badly. Making her own damn world was the only thing that remained to be done.

WELCOME TO DOLLYWOOD

25 years after constructing an amusement park in her native Smoky Mountains, Parton told Maverick magazine, "I never got to go to Disneyland as a child, but I was always captivated with it. In the 1980s, Parton had fled the Smokies to establish a location named Dollywood because she was homesick and dissatisfied with the Hollywood she had imagined as a child.

The Dollywood theme park wasn't just an egocentric business. It was her plan to revitalize the depressed rural economy of her hometown and employ its residents, including her own family.

Parton was in charge now, and her business judgment was sound. She admitted to Reuters that her investment in Dollywood, which celebrated its 30th anniversary in 2016, was her most successful one. Every year, three million people come. The fact that several generations of Parton's own family members continue to work and perform at the attraction, as she had envisioned, adds to her satisfaction and, in reality, to the success of the park.

Parton's objectives for Dollywood's influence on the community were also successful. According to a study conducted by University of Tennessee academics this year, the tourist hub in Pigeon Forge, Tennessee, employs roughly 3500 people and generates close to 20.000 jobs in the region along with two associated attractions. The study calculated that Dollywood's annual economic impact on East Tennessee is $1.5 billion. (That is a billion, yes.) Not only would Parton have missed out on financial gains, but an entire state would have as well, had she listened to those who questioned her commercial acumen.

Despite the beginning of that project, Parton was able to collaborate with Emmylou Harris and Linda Ronstadt on one of the finest albums of all time, Trio, which was released in 1987. Trio, which has amazing harmonies and a decidedly country flavor, was nominated for a Grammy and topped the Billboard country albums chart.

Parton presented a brand-new TV program for ABC that same year. This time, Parton was criticizing someone else's ideas, and with good reason: they were awful. The show Dolly, which she had thought would be a more expensive version of the program with the same name that she hosted in Nashville in the 1970s, was compelled to air foolish, embarrassing skits by network television executives. Her innate talents for music, storytelling, and spontaneous discussion with guests were highlighted on that earlier broadcast. However, ABC insisted on certain things, like having her take a bubble bath on camera at the beginning of each episode of her new show. In her autobiography Dolly, she discussed what it was like to collaborate with a room full of male writers and producers:

Parton defended herself and her intentions for the show in an interview with co-host Charlie Gibson on Good Morning America in 1987 over the ratings issues with her new show.

Gibson never gave her a chance to promote her work in the segment. Instead of saying good-bye when he sealed her departure, Parton named the guests who will be appearing on her forthcoming program, including Patti LaBelle.

In the same year, Washington Post reporter Jacqueline Trescott included another Parton interaction into an article about new recruit Gibson's unimpressive presence next to Good Morning America co-host Joan Lunden. This was a rare instance of a media person highlighting Parton's wit rather than her body.

Regarding her TV program, Parton also had the final laugh. Because of a carefully crafted contract, ABC had to pay her millions to axe the program when ratings plummeted. She also left with a deeper understanding of the business world, which she detailed in Dolly: My Life and Other Unfinished Business after a rare occasion of going against her normal diplomatic manner and going for the throat. She cautioned not to believe the men in suits know what they're doing and not to worry about their opinion of your value.

Parton's professional approach to that challenge was to use it for her personal gain.

Parton was in full bloom as the 1980s came to an end as the lady we know today: a shrewd businesswoman with a hypersexualized physical presence she had carefully created for her own power and pleasure. She needed to turn a man's head at that point. She had been the boss for a while and was approaching forty.

She staged the tryouts for the male lead in a music video in her 1989 music video for "Why'd You Come in Here Lookin' Like That," from her legendary album White Limozeen, in a corny but endearingly satirical way. She didn't create the number-one single, which she now sings with conviction at the age of 71 and laments how good a bad boy's ass looks in "painted-on jeans." However, in the movie, she is in charge and is sitting in a darkened theater seat with the house lights out as she watches as guys enter the stage, flex their muscles, and play caricatures of all types of jerks. She smiles and still cares for them. She replies to the casting director, "I think they're all real sweet," when he asks her opinion. For her Christian patience, she received: A push broom-wielding, flawlessly sculpted janitor in cowboy boots and a cut-off denim shirt stumbled into the spotlight. Parton looks the janitor up and down as if to say, "You're hired," perhaps as a response to Charlie Gibson, Johnny Carson, Ronnie Milsap, and all the other strong, famous men who overlooked her artistic talent in favor of criticizing her physique.

MEDIA SCRUTINY

At a press conference in 1983 while Parton was in the UK for a TV special titled Dolly in London, a male reporter questioned her about whether or not she saw herself as a sex symbol. She explained that she didn't dress a certain way for attention, but rather because she was "impressed with the people back home"—a reference to the "trashy" ladies she had desired for their makeup and hair dye in a rural village where few women had access to such things because of both poverty and religious law. She delighted in being able to paint the painting she could now afford.

After jokingly mentioning Best Little Whorehouse and several rounds of laughter, a female journalist earnestly inquired about Parton's thoughts on sex work two questions later. Apparently feeling something accusing in the question or its timing, the group of reporters gasped. Parton's smile softened a little, and she paused before responding.

The "old boys" for Parton took many different shapes, including Hollywood directors, Nashville producers, and media interviewers. But as the British female journalist demonstrated, Parton's interactions with women were frequently equally problematic.

Parton was performing at a rodeo in Kansas City when Walters caught up with her in 1977 for an episode of The Barbara Walters Special. Parton's great celebrity had not yet outgrown this type of performance. On the tour bus she shared with her band when she was thirty-one and starting her pop music crossover, Walters conducted an interview with Parton. Walters questioned her about a variety of topics during their conversation, including whether there was any "hanky panky" between Parton and her band, whether she reached puberty early, whether she had real breasts, why she wore tacky wigs and makeup, and how she could possibly keep a husband from leaving her while she was constantly on the road. I have better things to do than to sit in my room wondering, "Oh, what's Carl doing tonight?" (Parton)

Parton continued by saying that the reason she could "piddle around" with her appearance and clothes in a way that made her feel in control—rather than trying to gain the favor of society—was because of her profound security in her skill, her goodness, and all the other things Walters didn't question her about.

The fact that the 1977 interview still disturbs people today indicates that women have made progress, at least in terms of how they are treated by the media. Even if women are still subjected to sexist questions, the majority of today's top talk show hosts wouldn't approach Parton so crudely; if they did, a horde of furious Twitter users would be right behind them.

Even understanding interviewers like Oprah Winfrey, whom Parton had a clear fondness and respect for, were obsessed with the actress's body. On her talk show in the late 1980s, Winfrey—who was no stranger to the audience's constant scrutiny of her body—had Parton stand up so that they could scrutinize her twice.

The sexist interview gauntlet received a male perspective from Phil Donahue.

Parton responded, using the same story about "female problems" that she had given Winfrey, "No, actually I can't have kids." The truth, Parton has acknowledged in recent years, was more complicated; prior to her partial hysterectomy, she had fantasized about having children but instead chose to concentrate on her career—a preference that at the time was so unacceptable for a woman of childbearing age that over the years, she occasionally avoided addressing it.

These interview time capsules are essentially a comprehensive list of all the questions successful women—from politicians to celebrities to any woman with a profession in the public eye—are asked whereas men aren't. They may reveal more about the cultural moment than they do about the interviewers.

Even more slowly than race or gender did socioeconomic class enter the American consciousness. When Walters inquired about Dolly Parton's childhood on her television show, Parton gave an earnest response about the log home, the Little Pigeon River, and the numerous kids. Then Walters intervened in a manner that I am familiar with: the upper-middle-class or wealthy woman downplaying the roots of a "poor" woman.

At least on television, Parton had a chance to answer in-person and hoped the editors would treat the recording fairly. Print was a far riskier proposition: talking to a writer, usually a man, and allowing him to write whatever he wanted.

The legendary country music writer Chet Flippo once revealed a middle-aged man's conquering fantasy about his time with Parton in a particularly cringe-inducing Rolling Stone article from 1977. He imagines the encounter as a date when she travels next to him in a convertible; he should have booked dinner arrangements, he tells her. Although it was customary for celebrities doing publicity on the road to mention that a few talks had taken place in her hotel room, he made sure to mention it. A reader would be wondering by the time he got to the quote about Parton's freshly emerging breasts as a child and the other kids pulling at her jacket to see underneath if he was simply making stuff up. Journalists for magazines at the time were not known for taking precise notes, and in this case, Parton was the victim of a wild male-writer escapade.

What would you do if you were Dolly Parton and had to endure decades of these ridiculous celebrity interviews? You accept a part in a movie where you can portray a member of the media. Parton plays a small-town woman who quits her unfaithful boyfriend and seeks out a new life in Chicago in the 1992 romantic comedy Straight Talk. She ends up working as a "psychologist" on a radio talk show while having to conceal her working-class upbringing and lack of a college degree.

Parton wrote in her autobiography that she enjoyed making Straight Talk more than other of her cinematic endeavors, in large part because director Barnet Kellman "was willing to share what he knew with me" and "had a nice way of doing it." Her inherent wit was given the chance to emerge, and the script frequently incorporated her own countryisms. She ends up at conflict with (and falling for) a cunning newspaper writer. In the same way that she had previously corrected a male employer in "9 to 5," reclaimed the joke about her breasts, and changed the word "Hollywood" into "Dollywood," she assumed control in "Straight Talk" and seated herself as the interviewer.

THE FREEDOM TO WORK

Parton had her first film part as Doralee in the 1980s' 9 to 5, and she may have found her most cherished role as Truvy, the lovable and feisty proprietor of a beauty parlor, in 1989's Steel Magnolias.

Director Herbert Ross "didn't particularly like me or Julia Roberts at the start and [he] was very hard on her," she claimed in her memoirs. I couldn't act, he said. Women of a certain generation would disagree. Tickets for a screening of the classic tearjerker in Austin in the spring of 2017" included little imitation hairspray bottles that the Alamo Drafthouse theater staff had dubbed "Truvy's." When the character appeared on television, the predominantly female audience cheered.

Co-star Shirley MacLaine recalled Parton as a remarkably laid-back presence despite pressures on set in a Garden & Gun piece from earlier this year.

It was really hot, according to MacLaine. "There was Dolly, wearing a wig that must have weighed 23 pounds, heels that were approximately two feet high, and a waist cincher that was no bigger than 16 inches around. She was the only person who didn't perspire. She never voiced any grievances. Never. The rest of us were always grumbling.

Robert Harling, a screenwriter, has the similar memory of Parton.
In the middle of August, when we were sitting outside on Truvy's beauty parlor's porch, we were filming a portion of the Christmas scene, Harling said. "There were a lot of stops and starts while we waited. Dolly was seated on the swing, and the women were decked out for Christmas. She was swinging, cool as a cucumber, wearing that white cashmere sweater with the marabou around the neck. Dolly, we're dying and you never utter a word,' Julia exclaimed. Why don't you have fun? Dolly replied, "When I was young and had nothing, I wanted to be rich and famous, and now I am," with a very contented smile. I won't complain about anything, therefore.

She isn't known to complain about the care I've described here, so perhaps that explains why. However, Parton offers a critique in her own style. In response to a question from Cineaste magazine in 1990, Dolly Parton didn't respond, "That male bosses are still assholes ten years after 9 to 5." Instead, she stood in for the offender to protect one of her castmates from sexism.

"Daryl Hannah surprised me greatly. She's stunning and as kind as can be, but what an actress," Parton remarked. "... I was unaware of the girl's amazing talent because I had always pictured her as the lovely, long-legged blonde, falling victim to the same kind of stereotypical thinking that irritates me when it occurs to me. Daryl has an intriguing intelligence and sense about her and takes her acting very seriously. Rare."

In this way, Parton was a skilled, "uneducated" representative of a movement that was associated with protest groups and college campuses. The majority of the women I knew growing up in rural Kansas don't know who Gloria Steinem is, but they can quote word-for-word from Dolly Parton's films from the late 20th century and see themselves in her.

The patriarchal institution of marriage, socioeconomic inequity that frequently accompanies motherhood, and reproductive rights are all topics Steinem covered in her novels. In 2014, Parton sent the same message to Maclean's: I've had the freedom to work, and I believe that's one of the reasons I've succeeded, according to Parton. "I never had kids, and I never had a husband who bitched about everything I did."

I'm roughly four years old and wearing a white tank top with the Ms. magazine logo in one of the stranger pictures from my childhood, a yellowed square taken around 1984. No one in my family subscribed to Ms., and I wasn't even aware of Gloria Steinem's pioneering publication until I was an adult with a college education, so the tiny children's clothing must have been purchased at a yard sale. However, there I am in 1980s rural Kansas wearing feminist clothing—I guess not because my mother wanted to make a point, but rather because it was on the five cents table in someone's Wichita driveway.

My fractured socioeconomic experience was somehow made whole by Steinem's or even someone repping her on social media praising a brief description of my mother: raised in abuse and poverty, seventeen when she became pregnant with me, tenacious as a worker paying the bills, intellectually and creatively gifted but unable to attend college, coveted as a woman deemed beautiful.

I was stunned by Steinem's explanation of how such virulent misogyny could dominate the 2016 presidential race that evening during her speech on the campus of the University of Texas. Steinem noted that when a woman flees, it is when she is statistically most likely to be killed by her male abuser. The unfathomable fear of losing control of her causes the aggressive ex-husband to lose his cool.

A patriarchy losing control of half the population of the United States would definitely explain a lot about recent years. The murder of abortionist George Tiller in Wichita in 2009, Hillary Clinton's treatment and defeat in 2016, and the consistent history of violence against and animosity against women among male perpetrators of this century's epidemic of mass shootings are all examples of this. It might also explain how a strong, independent lady like Dolly Parton ends up being made fun of.

Similar to Steinem, Parton is a symbol of 20th-century American womanhood who is still active today, possibly with the same vigor that other women of a similar age who chose more conventional paths must provide for their future generations. Steinem did not come from a wealthy family, but the two ladies experienced social status differently: one went to college and the other traveled to Nashville with a guitar. They both paved the path for us to nominate a woman for president in 2016 in distinct ways and with different strategies.

When a woman eventually wins the presidency, she'll be subjected to the same sexist media inquiries as Hillary Clinton, Dolly Parton, and Gloria Steinem have, and she'll get attacked for her choices and appearance just like they all have. She will recall a time when she had to deal with males wielding some form of authority, whether it was the body-shaming Parton endured in Hollywood, the harassment Doralee endured in exchange for a job, or the doubts accountants on her own payroll cast upon her. She will be the first female boss in this nation, and the challenges of being a woman will inevitably shape her leadership.

The triumphant female employees in 9 to 5 reconstruct the entire office with a frenzy of overdue raises, recognition for cubicles full of women, and some productivity-enhancing décor to boot while their boss is collared and chained in his own bedroom.

We must allow women the ability to practice feminism whatever they see fit, whether we agree with it or not, so that some females may have the opportunity to similarly reorganize this failing democracy. When Sanders ran against Clinton in the 2016 primaries, women disparaged his female supporters, which is similar to how Barbara Walters criticized Dolly Parton's fashion choices in 1977.

If Parton's difficulties and achievements as an implicit rather than an explicit feminist have taught us anything, it is that the politics of a movement do not always correspond with the most true forms of female power. I would hazard a guess that Parton's feminism has aged equally as well, if not better, than some of the statements and writings made and published by activists, academics, and other movement-approved experts from the same era.

For our collective good, a generation of women who will soon hold positions of authority have profited from both, whether directly or indirectly. They weren't all able to attend college, but they are all the daughters of people who work a 9 to 5 job—the kids whose lives may be used to chart Dolly Parton's transformation from a country singer to a business empress to a global icon. They are old enough to recall having record players in every home yet young enough to have been influenced by hip-hop. They are old enough to have divorced but young enough to still get asked when they will finally have a child. They witnessed their mothers being patronized and abused so that perhaps a later generation wouldn't have to, and they are now prepared to reverse the progress that anti-feminist reaction has achieved over the course of their lives. The three ladies who are now disgruntled at work are prepared to band together and hog-tie the male supervisor until they receive some goddamn respect.

A revenge fantasy, according to some, 9 to 5 is what I consider to be a parable about justice. They don't want to see their employer suffer; they want to be treated fairly, which is merely misandry in the eyes of male privilege.

She told the crowd that the fired drummer had scowled at the show's outfits. Instead of a Vegas mega-show, it was intended to be a basic, understated production that evoked a front porch in Tennessee. Yet here was Dolly wearing her customary rhinestones, big hairstyle, and shoes. He advised her to make her outfit simpler as well.

Parton has a knack of being cautious with details and is an expert at controlling what the public learns. Although Parton has been successfully running her own music productions for decades, her narrative about a male employee offering her advice on her stage presence seemed accurate, and it was obvious that she enjoyed telling a tale about being the boss.

She undoubtedly remembers how she used to be. She shared a black-and-white photograph of Wagoner giving a valuable piece of jewelry to her twenty-something self in her book Dolly; the young Parton is sporting a beehive wig and a tight, obedient smile. The picture has the text, "Me and Porter: Oh boy, a ring, but what I wanted was a raise."

In the end, Parton received much more than a raise; she also received the entire world, and it appears that the drummer she hired for this tour was unaware of this. She gave him the two words that every woman ought to have the opportunity to utter: "You're fired."

Chapter 4:
Cements Her Icon Status

Dolly Parton reunited with her 9 to 5 co-stars Jane Fonda and Lily Tomlin to present an award at the 2017 Emmy Awards. All three of them received Emmy nominations: Fonda and Tomlin for their performances as upper-class friends in Southern California in the Netflix comedy series Grace and Frankie, and Parton for her work as a producer on the 2016 television film Christmas of Many Colors, in which she portrays an Appalachian sex worker.

Fonda emphasized Parton and Tomlin's position as sage feminists while they were on stage together.

Parton said, "I'm just hoping that I'm going to get one of those Grace and Frankie vibrators in my swag bag tonight," in reference to a season two plot point from their show.

Her response was the least overtly political of the trio. It was also the one that was most likely to irritate a man like Donald Trump, who believes that women exist for his pleasure, lose worth as they get older, and require a man in order to experience sexual satisfaction. What could be more anti-Trump than a wealthy woman in her seventy-ones on national television dreaming about a sex object once his name was mentioned?

Because their imaginary office boss was elevated to the position of world leader in that feminist film, the stars were forced to confront the past in the present.

The country music industry is seeing a swing backward in opposition to advancements made for women in the late 20th century, just like the rest of the country, where conservatism now controls the law and the White House. According to Forbes magazine, less than 10% of country radio airplay in the first half of 2016 were songs performed by female singers. Only five female musicians could be found on Billboard's Top 30 Country Airplay charts at the same time.

The previous year, influential country radio analyst Keith Hill gave an explanation of why stations continue to have a disproportionate number of men on the air. "Take females out of country radio if you want to make ratings," Hill advised Country Aircheck. He claimed that women "just aren't the lettuce in our salad." Luke Bryan, Blake Shelton, Keith Urban, and similar performers make up the lettuce. The female tomatoes in our salad are there.

The remark spurred a long overdue debate on a long-standing issue, and female artists voiced their displeasure. To raise money for her organization, Martina McBride sold "tomato" shirts. Jennifer Nettles wrote on Twitter that the opportunity was "big old vagina-shaped" at the time.

Men and women in the music industry backed Hill's remark with justifications based on statistics and data: When the numbers are crunched, even female listeners prefer male performers since there aren't enough good female albums, female songs don't test as well, and so on. But this wasn't always the case. Whatever the causes, the results speak more to current cultural attitudes than they do to the caliber of women's music.

Female performers were flourishing in the industry when Dolly Parton last had a solo number-one success with "Why'd You Come in Here Lookin Like That" in 1989, paving the way for Reba, Faith, and Shania's glorious 1990s. However, a recent Stanford University study found that women had slid off the charts since the beginning of the millennium, despite record labels continuing to promote new female musicians.

Parton has explained her own absence from the charts as a result of her advanced age as an artist. She explained to Rolling Stone in 2003, "When the new country came along, any artist over thirty-five was thought to be a has-been." And, Lord, I've been here so long that I've become something of a legend. But I was far from finished. I thought I was doing better than ever. I think I'm only now getting experienced enough to know how to operate in this industry. "Well, hell," I said to myself, "I'm not going down with the rest of them old farts." I'm going to come up with some fresh approaches. And I actually did just that.

At age 48, Parton established her own record company at a time when pop music dominated the country music scene. She told Rolling Stone, "Now that I don't have fourteen managers and record executives telling me you gotta be more commercial, you gotta be more pop, I thought, 'Well, now I can record the songs I truly want to. 'I don't care if I create [a song that is] six or seven minutes long—I'm going to tell the story,' I reasoned. I won't be thinking, "Oh, I need to reduce this to fit the radio." Fine if they broadcast it on the radio. Don't care anymore and doubt they would.

Young female singer-songwriters today who emulate Dolly Parton's style—old twang, contemporary concepts, gothic country themes, and spiritual vulnerability—earn positive reviews, sell records, and fill venues. However, such musicians—including indie darling Valerie June, emerging star Kacey Musgraves, and superstar Miranda Lambert—work in a field that is currently betting against them.

KEEPING IT REAL

Parton has demonstrated a devotion to honesty over commercial success with her late-career choices. Parton has released more than a dozen solo albums of brand-new music since going independent with her own label in the early 1990s. Some of it is wholly bluegrass, including a 2001 rendition of Collective Soul's rock song "Shine" that earned her a Grammy. It was released at the same time when polished pop country acts like Keith Urban and Rascal Flatts were taking over the radio.

However, the music from the earlier part of her career continues to be her signature, and a generation born after Parton stopped appearing on country radio is now discovering it. With her large hairdo 1970s picture on devotional candles in chic shops and online shopping carts, it appears to them that she is more than simply an entertainment; she is a spiritual patron. It seems appropriate to refer to Dolly's current position as "one of the few living astral moms," a term that a friend of mine recently used to describe a well-liked public radio broadcaster.

Whether or not Dolly Parton has another game-changing success, her entire life is now recognized as having made history—for female artists, for underprivileged girls with dreams, and for women who want to be bosses without covering their breasts. This late discovery of Parton was a slow process, but the 2014 Glastonbury Festival in England may have been the turning moment.

In the early 2000s, Parton engaged Nashville manager Danny Nozell to assist in planning a tour after going seventeen years without a manager. Nozell developed a strategy to promote her writing to young people all across the world. Her 2007 European tour, 2008 arena tour, and two 2018 Australian tours were all sold out. But from 2006 to 2013, Parton declined pleas to perform at Glastonbury, a massive festival that is distinctly rock and roll. She thought the festival wouldn't be a good fit, according to an interview she gave to the Guardian in 2014. Her devoted fan following has been international for decades.

Even Dolly Parton was in the dark when she eventually made the leap in 2014 to headline Glastonbury: Her performance drew an estimated 180,000 spectators, the largest festival audience ever and more than a Rolling Stones concert. The BBC broadcast the festival live to a record-breaking viewership of 2.6 million viewers.

Glastonbury was far from the East Tennessee farm where Parton performed for the hogs as a young child using a tin can as a makeshift microphone. The song "Mud," which she wrote for the infamously muddy festival, paid homage to her farm's roots despite the fact that she had left it fifty years before for the large international audience. Parton claimed, "This muck ain't nothing new to me. I grew up on a farm.

Working with much younger musicians has been a key component of Parton's current success in attracting new followers. Parton performs a duet of "Old Flames (Can't Hold a Candle to You)," written by Kesha's mother Pebe Sebert, on the pop singer Kesha's most recent album, which was released in August. Brandi Carlile's "The Story," which was originally recorded by Dolly Parton, was covered for an album earlier this year to raise money for a charity that helps refugee children. Her "Jolene" recording, which was reworked by the up-and-coming a cappella group Pentatonix, won her the 2017 Grammy for Best Country Duo/Group Performance.

Miley Cyrus is Parton's goddaughter, and she has long supported her, making appearances on her Disney TV show, inviting her onstage, and even performing with her on The Voice, maybe to their mutual benefit. An acquaintance of mine who works in journalism once recalled how he and Hugo Chávez were watching the World Cup in a pub in Venezuela when Chávez's daughter told him that she and her friend were big fans of the "new Miley Cyrus song" about a woman named Jolene. They were awestruck when he played a video of the Parton original on his phone to them.

Many members of the new fandom might only be able to name five Parton songs, but there will be lots of opportunities for them to learn more because of how diverse Parton is. Such diverse superstars as Patti Smith and Kitty Wells have recorded her songs. Her films include those that are now regarded as masterpieces, most notably 9 to 5 and Steel Magnolias. Late-career Parton, however, is much more; she is a charitable force and a voice for the progressive cause in traditionally conservative circles.

According to the organization, her literacy program, Imagination Library, has sent more than 80 million books to more than one million kids worldwide.

While her open Christian faith and use of the common vernacular have helped her build a connection between crossover fans and the underprivileged, rural South, her outspoken progressivism regarding gay and transgender rights, gender parity, and other topics has forced country music to adapt.

The University of Tennessee presented a history course in the fall of 2017 that used Dolly Parton's biography to study Appalachia in the twentieth century, from child labor regulations to current economic challenges. She has both a rose and a movie named after her—the independent 2015 film Seeking Dolly Parton. As Oprah Winfrey is to journalism, Parton is now to country music what she was to the media: a natural talent who, by being herself, transcended a field to change society.

Women's advancement in country music was a part of the change she oversaw; although Nashville is still deeply ingrained in sexism, progress has been made since she arrived in the 1960s.

Perhaps because of her appearance and persona, however, Parton had not previously received the same respect from music critics and Hollywood as, for example, Loretta Lynn, whose life was the subject of the Oscar-winning biopic Coal Miner's Daughter and whose music inspired the adoration and collaboration of indie darling Jack White.

However, when viewed in the context of the twenty-first century, with young fans and more women in the media that shapes the narratives about her, Parton's place in culture eventually transforms from the divine feminine—a sassy priestess in high heels—to the objectified female body.

GIVING BACK

Parton started the Imagination Library in 1995, and she has stated that working with the children who receive free books in the mail every month, from birth to age five, is one of her greatest professional delights. She told PBS NewsHour in 2013 that the youngsters dubbed her "the book lady," unaware of her fame. This fall, Parton published her debut children's album.

When Dolly published her own children's book, I Am a Rainbow, in 2009, Parton told Time magazine, "Children have always responded to me because I have that cartoon-character look. "I sound small and overly exaggerated, and I kind of resemble a Mother Goose character," Dolly said.

Her interest in reading was sparked by the illiteracy of her father, Lee. The Little Engine That Could, with its lessons on perseverance and hard work, may be the first book given to each kid in the program because of this familial background, which is thought to be the reason for Dolly Parton's legendary rise out of poverty. At Dollywood's Imagination Playhouse, the story has been presented live, bringing to life many of the program's choices.

Imagination Library, which is frequently supported by local libraries, only needs a simple form with an address and the child's birth date to confirm age eligibility. No income paperwork or other hoops need to be jumped through. The Dollywood Foundation's choice shows that someone in the organization understands what it's like to be a child in need. Since everyone is eligible, the most vulnerable kids can profit without feeling bad about using a poor people's program.

Similarly devoid of bureaucracy was Parton's relief effort for Smoky Mountain wildfire victims last year. The Dollywood Foundation offered affected households, whether they were homeowners or renters, $1,000 every month for six months in exchange for simple proof of address. The Tennessean published footage of an interaction with one beneficiary at the conclusion of that time period, in May of last year, when Parton made a statement and visited some of the 900 families who had benefited.

She donated $3 million to start the Mountain Tough fund, which enables social workers to get low-income fire victims things like transportation to work and medication for health issues brought on by fires, in order to meet the long-term needs of individuals who lost their homes and more.

I've seen shocked reactions to Dolly Parton's charitable work, which includes sending millions of books to kids, raising millions of dollars for fire victims, awarding decades' worth of high school scholarships to Tennessee seniors, and founding a foundation for healthcare in 1983 and naming it after the rural doctor who delivered her. One can only think that other renowned people are as giving as she is. However, I've never witnessed somebody more shocked to learn about celebrity generosity as when they read about Dolly Parton's.

This might be the case given that Parton has donated the majority of her time without a public ceremony or news release, just a quiet check and her name on a board of directors. For nearly thirty years, Imagination Library in particular maintained a low profile, which must have been Parton's preference at the time. But in a 2009 documentary about the book program, children's author Robert Munsch, who was featured, got to the heart of the matter—namely, why her goodness is such a revelation.

BIG BUSINESS

The size of Parton's commercial empire may not be well known to the general public either. She has published music, books, movies, TV series, and even ventured into restaurants over the years. In 1986, she and her manager Sandy Gallin co-founded Sandollar Productions. Blockbuster hits like the 1991 comedy Father of the Bride and the television series Buffy the Vampire Slayer are just two examples of the company's accomplishments. Other cultural milestones include the 1989 AIDS film Stories from the Quilt, which received the Academy Award for best documentary.

Parton's ongoing Dollywood entertainment park in Pigeon Forge outperforms even blockbuster Hollywood success financially.

In a 2009 article for National Geographic Traveler, author Keith Bellows, who spent fifteen years living in East Tennessee, attested to the attraction's strong ties to the community.

The area was formerly a Silver Dollar City facility with a rustic Ozarks motif, designed after a park in Branson, Missouri. Since Parton changed the park in 1986, her influence can be felt everywhere; there is even a museum dedicated to her and a copy of the home she grew up in.

While many theme parks cultivate a fantastical ambiance meant to transport guests to another location filled with mythical characters, Parton's inspiration was to emphasize the natural surroundings and working people who created her—keeping it local before local was popular. Parton said to Bellows, "I'm keen to keep the character of the town. "To appreciate God's beauty, that means take a beautiful walk, smell the air, feel the temperature, cling onto the present now, take a drift on a trail, and gaze intently into the stream. That has far greater meaning than all the world's fabrications combined.

Country music expert Pamela Fox noted that Dollywood not only promotes the Smoky Mountains for the rest of the globe but also supports that region's poorest people in the context of their own homes in 1998 when analyzing country music autobiographies in the academic journal American Quarterly. Fox stated that Parton insists that the business honors 'her people' by employing mostly real hillbillies' to portray mountain culture, chastising those opponents who dismiss the theme park as a vanity endeavor. She simultaneously designed the park to evoke vintage, small-town carnivals, the ostensible Other of that impoverished society.

Even with the best of intentions, a cynic would argue that Parton has used the rural poor, a socioeconomic and geographic Other, to her own advantage. One could argue that by hiring locals, Dollywood is forcing them to act in aspects of their real lives, just like previous cultures and entire races have been forced to do for more affluent people in exchange for money and survival. But with Dollywood, Parton was and still is a native of the area.

As a white person who grew up in rural poverty, I won't use the word, but Parton frequently makes jokes about being "white trash," which she has earned the right to say. Either directly resist degradation or seize its means are viable options; Parton favors the latter. She became wealthy, returned home, and, before wealthy metropolitan developers could, transformed Appalachia into a show to combat the dehumanization of the rural poor. It's similar to how she always makes a joke about her breasts before a male talk show host does.

Dollywood, which is a mere few miles from the place where Parton was born, is evidence of Parton's fidelity to her people, not just in the shared past but also in the present. She writes their checks, pays for their high schoolers' college tuition, contributes to a foundation to cover their medical expenses, and organizes telethons when wildfires destroy their homes. All employees have access to an on-site health care clinic, and full-time employees of the park enjoy extensive health insurance benefits, despite the fact that earnings at the amusement park are ordinary for that sector of the economy (poor hourly pay for seasonal recruits like students on summer break).

Make no mistake: Parton set out to become wealthy and enjoy her wealth, and she has succeeded in doing so. She made the Forbes list of the top 100 highest-paid artists in the world this year for the first time, coming in at number 71, ahead of Rihanna, Billy Joel, and Katy Perry. This was made possible by the sustained success of Dollywood and her 2016 tour.

She claims that her money hasn't altered her taste. According to Parton, she and her husband enjoy traveling in an RV and grabbing food from drive-through windows at fast food restaurants.

She revealed to Billboard in 2014 that she had a passion for real estate. "It's not to say, 'Hey, look at me,'" she clarified. "I'd rather buy a house than trade stocks." She owns two homes in Tennessee and one in Los Angeles. (One can speculate that she conceals more than what she publicly discloses.)

Similar to every other area of her profession, a large portion of her real estate holdings are situated in her home state. She could afford to look chic and smart, but she has stuck with a look that is based on her idea of glamorous poverty. She might modify her speech while with people of higher social strata, but she keeps saying "ain't." She could discuss and sing about her decades of extraordinary experiences, her journeys throughout the world, but she prefers to focus on the impoverished people who brought her. According to Jancee Dunn's 2003 article for Rolling Stone, "Many people who are raised in near-poverty try to distance themselves from their upbringing, but not Parton, whose ticket out turned into a round-trip."

This journey is made both in spirit and in the physical body. The park is well-known for having Parton physically present, whether for an event or to visit one of her own shops. "I love Dollywood, because I love to go shopping up there in the stores," she said to

Dunn. 'Oh, excellent, I don't have to pay for this,' I think. I'm abusing my own position.

HITS AND MISSES

Even though she is self-aware and intelligent, Parton's career and empire are not without flaws. 2018 will mark the 30th anniversary of Dixie Stampede, a dinner theater experience that is one of Parton's biggest commercial headaches.

The daily event includes horse-riding acrobatics like barrel racing and musical shows while spectators consume chicken with their fingers. It is held in a 35,000 square foot rodeo arena with seating for more than a thousand people. Dixie Stampede is a very patriotic event with a hefty dose of white-washed nostalgia for the Antebellum South, in contrast to Parton's message, which is typically a class-conscious advocacy for love and acceptance. Customers are asked to select which side they will support during the event, which has the Civil War as its main focus.

Dollywood's home town of Pigeon Forge, as well as a nearby water park, and a second location in Branson, Missouri, are among the locations. Another was open for eighteen years in Myrtle Beach, South Carolina, before Parton invested $11 million to turn it into a dinner theater with a pirate theme the following year. In 2003, a less successful facility opened adjacent to Disney World in Florida; it closed five years later.

The remaining Tennessee and Missouri facilities had a $2.5 million renovation in 2015 that featured fresh sound effects and music. By that time, more than 20 million individuals had accessed Parton's website.

Years before that upgrade, my family and I visited the Branson facility, and we found it to be very different from Parton's in both spirit and actual presence. Several times during the performance, a tape of Dolly Parton's voice came through the speakers, implying that she would make an appearance. I found this annoying and demeaning to the intelligence of the audience members.

Regarding the spectacle itself, I used to enjoy a good barrel race just as much as the next gal because I attended rodeos as a child. But I was in college when I waited in line at Dixie Stampede, studying about the crucial role that Kansas, my home state, played in starting the Civil War by declaring itself a free state. Kansas still maintains a tense relationship with Missouri due to the bloodshed at the border of the Confederacy-glorifying Missouri during that time. It's possible that's why, even as a very naive and privilege-oblivious young white woman, I wasn't really charmed with a plot that sanitized the Civil War for the sake of corny amusement.

After the refurbishment, in August of last year, Aisha Harris, a culture journalist for Slate, wrote a long awaited review of Dixie Stampede in which she criticized it as a "lily-white kitsch extravaganza that play-acts the Civil War but never once mentions slavery." The South isn't represented by the Confederate flag, but a gray banner evokes the hue of that army's uniforms. The final message of the show is that there is only one United States of America, and we are all its citizens.

Harris observed surprise at the presence of individuals of color in the audience and among the staff after attending two 2017 performances to gather information for her work. However, she thought the performance was a frightening, irrational spectacle.

Harris, who admitted to being a Parton fan, emphasized that this regrettable aspect of Parton's career served as an example of the denial that permits white people to support Confederate monuments or to view anti-racism demonstrations and white nationalist rallies as morally comparable.

A few weeks after her article was published, Harris revealed for Slate that she had contacted Dixie Stampede for a reaction and received an email stating that they would "evaluate" her work.

Harris kindly conveyed her hope that the company would actually change in a follow-up interview with Slate, despite the fact that the company's initial response could be characterized as lackluster. She added, "It's great to hear that my assessment might push the show's writers to reevaluate its framing and presentation as a fan of Parton's other work in movies and music and as someone who believes that it matters how honestly we tell our nation's history.

When one considers that Parton has over the years taken courageous stances for the LGBTQ community, for women, and for the underprivileged, one can see how upsetting this disrespectful portrayal of brutal history is. Her message of love has stayed consistent across the board in regards to everything else, including race and political allegiance. Now, a contentious political period just so happens to coincide with Parton's late-career force and presence. How will she utilize it?I

Parton at least made passing mention of the divisive 2016 presidential election as well as the racial-related police shootings and rioting onstage during her 2016 tour. Before singing a touching selection of folk songs that were popular at the last time our culture was at such a boiling point—the beginning of her career, the tumultuous 1960s—she made reference to the nation's unstable state.

She sang "If I Had a Hammer" and other counterculture standards while her unplugged musicians joined her on an upright bass, guitar, and tambourine. She was decked out in rhinestones and held forth with the strong voice from her diaphragm that I've always preferred to the soft, girly voice she affects for some of her hits. Many people in the audience joined in, some of them crying.

NIP IT, TUCK IT, SUCK IT

Sometimes aging superstars must face a moral reckoning. Do their behaviors and morals withstand the test of time as civilization changes? In the sexist milieu of his youth, Bill Cosby's claimed serial rapes II went unpunished, but they are now the stuff of career ruin. As public opinion toward the Vietnam War became increasingly critical, feelings toward Jane Fonda's anti-war protests, for which she was demonized for decades, has shifted.

Physical aging is a further test in the development process for female stars. Parton is well known for having had a lot of plastic surgery and is open about it. She aspires to portray vitality because she thinks she has a reputation to uphold. In her 1994 autobiography, she stated, "I have done it and would do it again when something in my reflection doesn't look to me like it belongs to Dolly Parton. "I believe I owe it to my audience and myself. If it is not necessary, my spirit is too lovely and vibrant to remain in an outdated body.

According to country music expert Pamela Fox's 1998 American Quarterly essay, Dolly Parton's poor childhood allowed her to feel at ease with a sense of detachment from her own body, which she had previously used for field work but now preferred to squeeze into costumes.

According to Fox, "Dolly Parton" becomes a distinct, almost reified character during the surgical reconstructive process that her body actually generates.... Parton is aware that gender performance includes having the appropriate hair color and fitting into an unrealistic hourglass figure. But she can pull off the performance with amazing success. She switches from the gender-based objectification of the present to the class-based objectification of the past. Her own unique "dream" is literally realized in the Dolly character.

When viewed in that context, a choice that some feminists might find absurd actually proves to be a success. She remarked, "I always said, if I see something sagging, bagging, and dragging, I'm going to nip it, tuck, and suck it," according to a 2004 interview with CBS. Do whatever is necessary. I mean, I almost think of myself as a show dog or horse. Always have had lovely boobs. When I was younger, I always had a lovely figure, but when I shed all that weight, I had them corrected and pumped up. Now all they do is stand there like courageous little warriors. They're incredibly huge, really expensive, and really mine right now.

In a civilization that managed to fixate so intensely on Parton's breasts that the first cloned mammal, a sheep made from a mammary-gland cell in 1996, was named after her, her sense of ownership over her body is a defiant gesture.

In response to the disparate treatment of male and female bodies, Parton chooses to mock men for their aging instead of embracing her own. Parton shared a well-known story of her song "Jolene" during a 2003 Crossroads series filming with Melissa Etheridge. Early in their marriage, a handsome bank employee caught her husband's attention, and Parton's song implored her not to take him.

She jokingly said, sitting next to Etheridge, "I look at him now, and I consider hiding his Viagra and saying, "Go get him."

Later in the set, the duo sang "Bring Me Some Water," a rock song from Etheridge's early career, which deals with envy. Tell me how will I ever be the same / When I know that woman is there screaming your name," Parton screamed while passionately singing the words. Parton abruptly created a younger man for her own delight as the song came to an end, changing her tone from pained to authoritative. Parton shook her head and exclaimed, "Hey, little water boy," with a palm on her hip. I said, "Bring the bucket around." Etheridge laughed aloud.

Her longtime friend and duet partner Kenny Rogers mentioned his own notoriously altered visage and how Parton had reprimanded him for it during an appearance with her on Good Morning America in 2013. Even if it was accurate, Rogers admitted that it was somewhat upsetting when the media focused on the whole plastic surgery issue. "Look, ol' Kenny's been to Jiffy Suck again," Dolly used to say.

He tried to draw away, but Parton sat next to him and grabbed his chin in her hand and looked at his face. She laughed and remarked, "I think he's really grown into his face-lift now, don't you?" He appears fantastic.

It is less amusing to regard Parton and Rogers' respective legacies differently.

Parton has penned countless songs, and her cultural influence is so great that in 2005 the National Endowment for the Arts gave her the National Medal of Arts, the highest award given in the nation for contributions to the arts. Rogers, on the other hand, became well-known by providing his soothing voice to someone else's words.

Many legendary musicians didn't write their own songs, yet Rogers has achieved a great deal in his career. But Parton's career helped him in his. Producer Barry Gibb said that they needed Parton to "make it pop" as Rogers was recording "Islands in the Stream" solo, as Rogers recalled on Good Morning America. The song has now become a staple of pop culture and one of the all-time best-selling duets. Although she didn't originate the song, Parton's presence beside him in the recording studio and on stage may have secured his legacy.

Despite all of this, Rogers—rather than Parton—became the second winner of the Willie Nelson Lifetime Achievement Award at the Country Music Awards (a year after Nelson himself won it in 2012).

The next year, Johnny Cash received the honor posthumously. Then, in 2015, when Parton became the fourth artist and first woman to get the honor, she endured the humiliation of having her acceptance speech cut short just as it was getting started.

Prior to performances of Parton's classics by Jennifer Nettles, Pentatonix, Reba McEntire, Kacey Musgraves, Carrie Underwood, and Martina McBride, co-star of 9 to 5 and friend Lily Tomlin gave a speech. One minute into her speech when Parton finally took the stage, the producers prompted her to finish.

SO MUCH SUBSTANCE

A woman's voice will be praised, but only to a certain extent, whether it be on the radio, on stage, or in a presidential election. There won't be much airplay. The speech will end quickly. Someone will shout, "Lock her up."

Parton, who is undoubtedly one of the least polarizing celebrities in pop culture, seems to encounter little direct hostility. But she has had to deal with the sexist pressure to be "likable" as a female CEO. 2014's "As a Southern woman, how do you speak your mind and take care of business but remain likable?" a question from Billboard was directed to her.

Parton didn't appear to be having sleepless nights due to the problem. "I'm open and honest," she said in response. "I don't take my time. I just say it if something is happening. I will occasionally use a few curse words to make my point when I'm angry. I frequently claim that I utilize my temper more often than I lose it. I adore peace and harmony, therefore I don't do either unless absolutely necessary, but if you walk into my area, I'll call you out on it. Oh, you simply seem so cheerful always, people say. That's the Botox, then.

The same glass ceiling that prevented Dolly Parton from answering more inquiries about her measurements than her music over the years also prevented Hillary Clinton from defeating a morally corrupt, incompetent guy in her campaign. The two women's journeys were significantly divergent. However, at almost the same age, they experienced something together: a breakthrough toward an equality that they individually would never experience.

Who will subsequently follow in Parton's footsteps and profit from her sacrifices? Many upcoming musicians cite Dolly Parton as an influence, but who could actually succeed her?

VH1 speculated that one such performer might be the hip-hop musician Nicki Minaj a few years ago. Jade Davis, a media critic, elaborated on the argument by pointing to Minaj's curvy body, big hair, and business expertise.

In fact, Parton contributed to the development of the kind of feminism that is prominent in modern pop music: offering out T&A on your own terms and resisting objectification by having a great time doing it. She also managed to accomplish this without necessarily sounding liberal America. 2015 saw a caller to CNN question Parton if she would identify as a feminist.

Oh, I'm a female and I firmly believe that everyone has the right to their own rights, she said. No matter your race, gender, sexual orientation, or gender identity, I don't care. Everyone who has something to contribute should be able to provide it and receive compensation, in my opinion. However, I don't identify as a feminist in the sense that some do because I only believe that everyone deserves respect.

If, like me, you speak the language of college-educated activists, her response can make you feel heartbroken. But I also speak of a poor country, and I can confirm that as a self-reliant kid in a small-town Kansas who believed that men and women should be treated equally, I might have provided a similar response. Our lack of a shared set of concepts is at the root of a great deal of our nation's current political problems.

Parton's gift to young women is not a claim within the context of her native class; rather, it is an illustration. One hopes a hero will provide both. But if I had to choose just one, I would choose the latter.

The pro-woman example set by Parton is still relevant to today's female creators. A young Dolly Parton admirer learns she is adopted in the 2011 Canadian film The Year Dolly Parton Was My Mom, which is set in rural Winnipeg in the 1970s. The feminist messages in the story are self-aware.

Just before Parton embarked on her tour, writer-director Tara Johns was able to deliver the script to her through a network of contacts in the hopes of using her music in the movie. According to Johns of the women's lifestyle website She Does the City, Parton responded with a faxed letter expressing that she had spent the weekend reading the script and was ecstatic. For a modest amount, Parton granted her permission to utilize nine songs, four of which were recorded by Canadian musicians for the soundtrack, including Nelly Furtado and the Wailin' Jennys.

Johns pointed out that because of how she went about it, Parton's groundbreaking feminism might have been disregarded. She took the entire objectification that most women complain about and threw it against the wall, according to Johns. And in a way, it's a challenge because she essentially refuted the notion and perspective on women as a whole. When the extremely thin exterior of that objectified image is removed, so much content is revealed.

Parton's picture experiments are not always so skillful. See her appearance on The Queen Latifah Show in 2013, shortly after Latifah starred in the all-Black female ensemble of the Steel Magnolias remake in 2012, in which Jill Scott played Dolly Parton's well-known beautician Truvy. Parton sang an original rap song while sporting an afro wig in what appeared to be a tribute to Latifah, with whom she co-starred in the 2012 musical film Joyful Noise.

"Hey, hoooo, hey, hoooo," was the standard hip-hop audience response before Parton burst into full East Tennessee: "I'm not calling anybody names. Simply saying, "How-deeee!"

She and Latifah both have enormous breasts, but only one of them is truly recognized for working them, Parton continued. She indicated her chest while wearing a skin-tight black leotard with long sleeves, just like she has done in recent years (it is said that she has numerous tattoos on her body).
She rapped, "Look at dem go!" about her breasts. Hey, I'm fiddling. I'm at work. I'm dancing. I've got your wrecking balls right here, Miley. A gasp that is a characteristic of Southern Protestant speech was added by Parton to the final word. She soon began humming above the beat, "She'll be comin' round the mountain when she comes."

It is uncomfortable to see the performance, which might have been the producer's idea. She evidently didn't realize that mentioning her affiliation with a "redneck mafia" in her invitation to Latifah to fight may make some viewers think of the bloody and brutal atrocities of white supremacy in the South. Parton's honest but clumsy purpose appears to have been to convey to Latifah's audience that she, too, was anOther" of sorts who was able to escape the role society had assigned her by acting in it.

Hip-hop referencing Parton is more effective than hip-hop referencing him. For instance, Minaj twerks while she calls out Miley Cyrus, the goddaughter of Dolly Parton, for cultural appropriation and challenges you to belittle her. She also makes sure her curves are in your face during the entire performance. She concludes her rap verse on Drake's song "Make Me Proud" with the command, "Double D up, hoes. Dolly Parton.

GOD'S LITTLE DOLLY PARTON
The fact that Parton has retained some of the girl she once was—not just as the star of a song about a coat made of rags, but also in her enduring sense of wonder about the world—is part of what gives her strength as a woman.

Dolly Parton talks about a fundamental delight for the natural world in one of the more shocking chapters in her book, Dolly: My Life and Other Unfinished Business.

Parton has simply described what she once knew as a youngster: the wild liberty of the impoverished child whose parents are hard at work while she amuses herself. This assertion could seem outlandish and doubtful in other celebrity autobiographies, but Parton has only recounted what she once knew. Parton's rural upbringing and the talent that made her stand out from other children meant that the Earth itself was her closest friend. It's simple to imagine that a celebrity famed for her groundedness has been simulating that feeling on a trail through her Tennessee estate.

This spirituality, which has been a part of Dolly Parton from her childhood and runs parallel to her Christian religion, is sensual, embodied, and unreliant on anyone or any particular belief system. She identified three loves in Dolly that had the most influence on her: sex, music, and God. The strict Pentecostal faith of her pastor grandfather, the homemade instruments she played barefoot on porches, and the twelve children her mother bore—likely due to a lack of contraception and a necessity for agricultural help—are all obvious in her rural East Tennessee upbringing.

Parton has refashioned and stitched these ideas together to create her own true life, just like her inventive mother did with a box of rags. Parton claimed sexual power while making a career out of music, not just in regard to a spouse but also in relation to everyone else, and she carried herself with a faith that manifests itself via Christianity but finds its strength internally rather than externally. ("The magic is inside of you," Parton has reportedly said. There isn't any sort of crystal ball.

Parton thought of producing a line of luxurious bras for ladies with large busts in her autobiography because she adored lingerie but was disappointed by its lack of options for her. Her next thought is a tender kiss-off to the pastor grandfather who had called her a prostitute for wearing makeup and tight clothing when she was a teenager. "Grandpa Jake is in heaven right now," she wrote. "I hope he's having fun watching me start a business selling the very things he used to reprimand me for," she said.

Parton has skillfully forced the world to face what patriarchy seeks to hide by telling the tale of her life through interviews, live concerts, books, and autobiographical TV movies.

Clarissa Pinkola Estés unearthed an archetype she said had been purposefully eliminated from myths, religious tales, and culture in her groundbreaking feminist book Women Who Run with the Wolves: Myths and Stories of the Wild Woman Archetype, published in 1992.

The erasure of female stories from foundational and historical books is echoed in the male executives' decision to exclude women from country radio. Both, as Parton's songwriting, personal experience, and profession show, can help a woman be heard. She serves as a contemporary representation of the rebellious woman, the Wild Woman of myth and feminism.

On the night of the 1989 Country Music Awards, that woman was gorgeous. Parton sang the Don Francisco gospel ballad "He's Alive," which she had previously sung on her White Limozeen album from the same year after being inspired by it one night on her tour bus. A tight white gown that wrapped her from neck to wrist to foot while she performed alone at the CMA concert clung to her contours. Her large blonde wig and glossy red lips were not modesty-inspiring.

The song recounts the events surrounding Jesus's resurrection from the perspective of Peter, who at first disbelieves Mary Magdalene, the female apostle who was the first to see Jesus alive when his tomb was discovered to be empty. As Mary had predicted, the tomb is empty when Jesus and John arrive, but they think the authorities have removed his body.

Parton sang the song at the CMAs with apprehension in her voice and on her face, her head cocked, and her eyes a little bit glassy, as if she were channeling the tune from a different source. As the story goes, Peter eventually witnesses the risen Jesus and is overcome with a sensation of peace, pleasure, and release. A bridge then altered the song's key.

Turning to face the audience and raising her arms, Parton demonstrated her revelation. A stage-widescreen was meant to rise behind her when she performed this, according to the plan. Then, after what looked to be a brief technical hiccup, Parton returned to the microphone and started the joyful breakthrough verse, "He's alive!" The screen finally appeared as she was doing so, presenting a sizable choir dressed in celestial robes that echoed "He's alive" higher on the scale.

When the camera went to the audience, at least one older man could be seen sobbing as the song so completely wrecked the auditorium filled with country music musicians.

Then, Parton appeared to grasp what had just transpired for a brief period of time. Welp, we just brought this bitch down, her face assumed a happy expression as her eyes grew clear and focused on the crowd. She swaggered backward with a swing in her hips and thanked the choir. She had just completed her professional goal, which was to let the world see her while simultaneously seeing God in a song.

DON'T NEED NO COMPANY

When Dolly Parton's long standing closest friend Judy left the Air Force early in her career, the two traveled to New York to live it up with Parton's fresh cash from The Porter Wagoner Show. According to her book Dolly, despite being a country TV celebrity, she could still manage to blend in with the crowd in New York City. Each of them carried a .38-caliber revolver in her purse as they donned tight skirts, lots of lipstick, and headed out on the town. Parton stated, "At the time, I believed carrying a gun was the right thing to do. I felt comfortable enough around one.

Around 1970, New York was grittier, and the women were country girls in their 20s with one goal in mind: to be terrible. They went in search of a dirty movie theater and sat down. However, this attempt at a small-scale innocuous controversy turned out to be awkward—two young women in a stench-filled auditorium with a number of males who were "the raincoat type." They were troubled by the film itself. In Parton's words, "what we thought would be exciting and sexy was gross, filthy, and insulting." Together with Judy, she left.

According to the book, they "dressed the way we were" and leaned against a wall to gather themselves a few blocks down the street. Parton was asked her hourly wage as a prostitute by a drunken man. She advised him to go off. The phrase "We don't need no company" was recalled by Parton.

As retaliation, he assaulted her by "grabbing at me in places I reserve for grabbers of my own choosing" and telling her she wanted it. Parton took her Smith & Wesson handgun from her purse before he could follow. She wrote, "As he walked away, I could hear him calling me a bitch.

A half-century later, Parton is just as well-known in New York and other parts of the world as she was in Nashville, and her entourage is armed. But the parable still holds true. Since then, she has challenged society with her confident demeanor and provocative image, raising the question "Am I asking for it?"

Parton discovered early on that people would perceive her as a cheap lady whose outward sexuality and looks demanded more instant attention than her creative output. Her mother would say to her, as she has stated on stage, "I hope you get a blessing out of it." Parton carried out that exact action with the unpleasant task society gave her.

She is therefore a paradoxical woman: a person with more class than most and a "trashy" demeanor. a family-oriented, self-described homebody who dresses "like a hooker". a bubbly blonde who is more intelligent than her male workers. a young child who "escaped" by singing about the location she left. a Christian who demonstrates authentic Christian behavior. A term of endearment that also connotes an inhuman thing made for another person's enjoyment, given to a woman of great depth who entered the world and was named after a toy doll.

She is a unique kind of icon, being both a sex symbol like Marilyn Monroe, a creative force like Loretta Lynn, and a charitable powerhouse like Oprah Winfrey. If Parton is a whore, then she is also the pimp turning herself out and the john enjoying it as she performs herself in the meantime.

Her tales of hard times were well received by the crowd, as always. But when she questioned whether or not she should run for president, the cheers were the greatest.

Parton is unlikely to be depicted in a presidential bust, but her hometown of Sevier County installed a bronze statue of Dolly in life size outside of its courthouse in 1987. She is depicted as a young woman with her hair pulled back, playing an acoustic guitar while perched on a rock. Her jeans are cuffed at the ankles to show her bare feet. This Dolly Parton is more like the one who runs through the woods than the one who performs in arenas wearing jumpsuits encrusted in rhinestones.

On Jimmy Kimmel's talk show in 2016, Parton stated, "After my dad passed away, one of my brothers told me that Daddy used to put a big oil drum of soapy water and a broom in the back of his truck."

And in the dead of night, he would descend to the statue and clean it completely of pigeon droppings.

Parton survived and even changed a man's world so brilliantly that one occasionally sees an unlikely reference to perhaps the most powerful, least political feminist in history on T-shirts or online memes. Whatever kind of icon she is, whatever she represents to her fans and the rest of society—a wax sculpture wearing sequined shoulder pads in a Los Angeles museum of celebrity likenesses, a barefoot bronze in East Tennessee, or a living national treasure who defies easy categories—Parton survived and even Parton recounted on Kimmel that her own father put the phrase "Dolly Parton for president" on a bumper sticker on his pickup.

Printed in Great Britain
by Amazon